Well Done

Finding and Fulfilling God's Plan for Your Life

By Mac Mayer

Well Done: Finding and Fulfilling God's Purpose for Your Life

By Mac Mayer

Copyright ©2016 by Mac Mayer (updated 2020)

All rights reserved. For use of any part of this publication, whether reproduced, transmitted in any form or by any means, electronic, mechanical, photocopying, recording, or otherwise, or stored in a retrieval system, without the prior consent of the publisher, is an infringement of copyright law and is forbidden. Names have been changed to protect the privacy of the individuals involved in the stories or scenarios. All other stories are composites of the lives of real people and any similarities to people you may know are purely coincidental.

The author and PUBLISHING CO. shall have neither liability nor responsibility to any person or entity with respect to loss, damage, or injury caused or alleged to be caused directly or indirectly by the information contained in this book. The information presented herein is in no way intended as a substitute for counseling and other forms of professional guidance.

To contact the author for speaking engagements, or for more information, you can access his website at www.macmayer.com

For large quantity orders call 1-877-750-4446

Scripture quotations marked (KJV) are taken from the King James Version Bible. The KJV is public domain in the United States.

Scripture quotations marked (NKJV) are taken from the New King James Version®. Copyright © 1982 by Thomas Nelson. Used by permission. All rights reserved.

Scripture quotations marked (AMP) are taken from the Amplified Bible. Copyright © 1954, 1958, 1962, 1964, 1965, 1987 by The Lockman Foundation. Used by permission.

Scripture quotations marked (ESV) are from the ESV® Bible (The Holy Bible, English Standard Version®), copyright © 2001 by Crossway, a publishing ministry of Good News Publishers. Used by permission. All rights reserved.

Front Cover Design: Chantel Miller
Cover Photo: Ashley Crandall
Interior Design: Robert Sweesy, Endurance Press

Print ISBN: 978-1-7335503-8-3

Library of Congress Control Number:
Printed in the United States of America

Published by Endurance Press

Table of Contents

Introduction 7

Chapter 1—The Message 11

Chapter 2—Primary Colors 20

Chapter 3—Traps 38

Chapter 4—Warning 52

Chapter 5—The Secret to Life 60

Chapter 6—Moving Forward Using Talents and Abilities 82

Chapter 7—I Am Responsible for Me 97

Chapter 8—Learning to Lead 112

Chapter 9—Pastors 130

Chapter 10—Some Final Thoughts: Team Up to Win! 144

Conclusion 151

Notes 153

Introduction

I had a blessed life. I was in my midforties, married to a beautiful godly woman, and was a multimillionaire with a large real estate portfolio. We lived in a two-story vintage country farmhouse with horses and cattle; we owned a vacation home at a world class resort, and had multiple cars, businesses, and the freedom to spend our time as we pleased. If the old adage "He who dies with the most toys wins" is right, we were excelling.

Then, within a very short time, a perfect storm of events hit, and everything we had spent our life building and accumulating was gone. My wife and I went from success to the verge of complete financial ruin and homelessness. It was then that I received a supernatural revelation that changed my life, and I believe will also change yours. This book explains this revelation and serves as a road map, a starting place, with specific actions to take that have helped us and countless others build lives of significance.

This book is prayerfully and specifically designed to give you practical, tangible steps to find and fulfill God's purpose and destiny for your life. We will expose some of the traps Satan uses to keep you from hearing, "Well done." Then you will discover the gifts and abilities God has specifically imparted to you. With the exciting discovery of knowing your gifts, you will proceed with definite steps to increase and utilize those abilities. As your journey continues, you will learn not only how to lead yourself but positively lead and influence

Acknowledgements

It is easy to discern from my story that without amazing people around me, I wouldn't achieve anything of value. Any success I have achieved comes first of all from my Lord and Savior Jesus, without whom I would be hopelessly and utterly lost, and secondly, from the incredible people I surround myself with. My wife and best friend Dianne has been a continual support and inspiration to me for decades. As far as staff is concerned, my main confidant for over 15 years has been the Legendary Mrs. Jenny Rupert. Words can't describe how much she has meant to Dianne and I. A special shout out and thanks to my long time Pastor and close friend Pastor Lynn Schaal of Amazing Grace in Twin Falls, Idaho who has been an amazing example of Christ through some of the toughest times of our life. Lastly, a gigantic thank you to Pastor Mark and Amy Boer who lead the thriving Life Church in Boise, Idaho. I'm continually thankful for your dedication and determination to go after all God has for you. Thanks to you all. I believe together we will hear "Well Done thou good and faithful servant."

others. Finally, you will learn how to use your abilities for a compounded effect by working with others, including pastors and churches, to influence multitudes for Christ.

At the end of every chapter, we have included specific questions that will assist you on your journey as you discover your gifts and how to use them successfully for the kingdom of God. Our goal is to help you live your life in a meaningful way, so you will receive the ultimate reward of a life well lived, when you hear, "Well done, thou good and faithful servant" (Matthew 25:21, KJV) from Almighty God.

We stand with you and pray God's greatest blessings for you to live a life of significance for the kingdom and ultimately hear, "Well done."

Mac & Dianne

> *His lord said to him, "Well done, good and faithful servant; you have been faithful over a few things, I will make you ruler over many things. Enter into the joy of your lord" (Matthew 25:23, NKJV).*

WELL DONE

Chapter 1—The Message

I was invited to preach at a local church, and I began working on my notes. I sat in my home office, staring intently into the Bible and listening as the Lord revealed to me what to teach. Slowly, a profound Presence came over me. It seemed like an invisible, thick fog had blanketed me. My body just relaxed as I became aware that something significant was slowly engulfing me with a warm, weighty feeling. I exhaled, leaned back, and intently shut my eyes. I "heard" a firm, clear Voice in my mind: "Mac, you have to tell them this message is serious. Many are planning on making excuses for how they are living and ultimately wasting their lives. They are already planning to place blame on something or someone else, instead of taking responsibility for their lives. Mac, I don't take excuses. There is nowhere in my Word where I accept excuses. I didn't accept excuses from Adam and Eve, and I'm not going to start accepting them now. Tell them."

The blood drained out of my face. The Voice had my full attention. The message was not threatening; it was very loving, yet resolute and firm. All I could do was sit and ponder the enormity of the moment. What does that mean—"tell them"?

I imagined myself as an Old Testament prophet. You know—long dingy robes, scraggly beard and unkempt hair, standing in a cloud of dust, yelling at a crowd who was so caught up in their lives that they did not want to hear a thing

I was saying. But I digress . . . robes are put away, hair is washed, and I direct my attention back to you, the reader. The Sunday morning message I was preparing that day was the Parable of the Talents.

Jesus was known for telling parables or stories that had deep, spiritual meaning. It seemed that He told these stories because not only were the messages timeless, but they were easy to remember and repeat for those who heard them. Remember that this was the pre-Internet and video podcast era, back to the time of scrolls written with sharpened sticks dipped in a crude ink mixture. Jesus told these stories to His followers, and they repeated them, wrote them down, and copied them until they were gathered in what became the Bible and passed down to you and me. The great thing about these truths that Jesus told is that they are just as relevant today as they were two thousand years ago.

The Parable of the Talents

For the kingdom of heaven is like a man traveling to a far country, who called his own servants and delivered his goods to them. And to one he gave five talents, to another two, and to another one, to each according to his own ability; and immediately he went on a journey. Then he who had received the five talents went and traded with them, and made another five talents. And likewise he who had received two gained two more also. But he who had received one went and dug in the ground, and hid his lord's money. After a long time the lord of those servants came and settled accounts with them.

So he who had received five talents came and brought five other talents, saying, "Lord, you delivered to me

WELL DONE

*five talents; look, I have gained five more talents besides them." His lord said to him, "***Well done***, good and faithful servant; you were faithful over a few things, I will make you ruler over many things. Enter into the joy of your lord." He also who had received two talents came and said, "Lord, you delivered to me two talents; look, I have gained two more talents besides them." His lord said to him, "***Well done***, good and faithful servant; you have been faithful over a few things, I will make you ruler over many things. Enter into the joy of your lord."*

Then he who had received the one talent came and said, "Lord, I knew you to be a hard man, reaping where you have not sown, and gathering where you have not scattered seed. And I was afraid, and went and hid your talent in the ground. Look, there you have what is yours."

But his lord answered and said to him, "You wicked and lazy servant, you knew that I reap where I have not sown, and gather where I have not scattered seed. So you ought to have deposited my money with the bankers, and at my coming I would have received back my own with interest. Therefore take the talent from him, and give it to him who has ten talents.

"For to everyone who has, more will be given, and he will have abundance; but from him who does not have, even what he has will be taken away. And cast the unprofitable servant into the outer darkness. There will be weeping and gnashing of teeth." (Matthew 25:14-30, NKJV; emphasis mine)

MAC MAYER

"Obvious" Answers

Some of the parables Jesus used had hidden meanings and others were more apparent. I think He made the Parable of the Talents easy to understand, yet many of us have missed its profound truth.

I remember as a child, my friends and I would try to mess with other kids by asking them questions with ultra-obvious answers, like "Who was buried in Grant's tomb?" The answer seemed so apparent that they thought it was a trick.

In the Parable of the Talents, Jesus, the Son of God said, "The kingdom of heaven is like . . ." I could read that and think, *Wow, isn't that a clever way of starting the parable; I wonder what idea Jesus is going to try to tell us about?* "Hello, Mac! Pay attention! I, Jesus, will be speaking very slowly. Actually for you Mac, I had it written down with words that aren't too big, and I have made the meaning quite direct. Try not to miss my point. **This is what the kingdom of heaven is like** . . . 'a man traveling to a far country, who called his own servants and delivered his goods to them.' Got it? **This is what the kingdom of heaven is like.**"

Okay, so it takes some of us a little longer to read and comprehend things, especially parables written over two thousand years ago. It is no wonder, considering that the average news article these days is between five hundred and eight hundred words and has a total shelf life of thirty-six hours. In this Information Age, some people wonder if there is really anything important that we could learn from a sixty-six-book piece of history. How could anything that was written so long ago be relevant to our lives today? Maybe there is something more profound and life changing we can find on TV or social media.

WELL DONE

Reality Show of Life

When I heard the Parable of the Talents, I thought of a reality show. Think *The Apprentice* meets *America's Got Talent*, only the stakes are much higher than big bucks or a residency in Vegas. In the story, we have four participants: the man traveling to a far-off country (aka the master—many people think he represents Jesus) and his three servants. In our analogy, I am going to refer to Jesus as the Reality Show Host—no disrespect intended. The reality show starts as the Host is preparing to leave, but not before He gives His three servants (whom I like to call contestants) some "talents." Then He rides off into the sunset.

The footnote in my NIV Bible says that talents equate to an amount of money. That sounds like a reasonable explanation, but what if the talents are literally meant to be natural abilities and skills? I am not trying to start an ancient conspiracy theory, and I know it is a stretch (understand I am not a biblical scholar), but humor me with the thought. The Host gives Contestant #1 five talents, Contestant #2 two talents, and Contestant #3 one talent. After He gives the contestants their talents, *poof!* He leaves the stage. **Game on**.

The game is not against each other. Each person is competing against himself. The basic premise of the game is to respond to the challenge and increase the talents with which they started. The Bible says the Host is gone a long time and then pops back in at an unannounced time to check on how the three contestants have done with what He left them. Does this sound like anyone you have heard about who will be coming back in the twinkling of an eye at an unexpected time? (Hint: check out Matthew 24:36–44.)

I'm Back!

When the Host gets back, He asks for an accounting from the people with whom He left His talents. Contestants #1 and #2 have doubled what they had, so He gives them an additional five talents and two talents, respectively. BONUS! Now that is what I call doing it right! Of course, their ultimate prize is not what they receive, but what the Host says to them: "Well done, good and faithful servant; you were faithful over a few things, I will make you ruler over many things. Enter into the joy of your lord" (Matthew 25:21, NKJV). Hmm, maybe I need to pay attention here. The reward is not the obvious extra talents, but a whole different way of seeing life.

Contestant #1 started out with two and half times what Contestant #2 originally received and the amount of their return is different, but they both get the same positive response: "Well done." Can you imagine Jesus saying "Well done" to you? Would you recognize that as the ultimate purpose for your existence? I don't think there could be anything better than Jesus looking at you with His amazing eyes of love and saying, "Well done. Enter into the joy of the Lord." I would take that over the biggest bag of money and a trip to Vegas any day! Let's be like Contestants #1 and #2.

Contestant #3 (Excuses, Excuses, Excuses)

I hate to spend any significant time talking about Contestant #3, mainly because I don't want anything to do with his mind-set or results. (Note to self: don't end up like Contestant #3.) Unfortunately, some people will give his lame excuses and ultimately hear a response from Jesus that is much worse than hearing, "You're fired," "You're out,"

"Good-bye" or "You've been chopped" as in a reality show. His response will be as it was to Contestant #3: "You wicked and lazy servant" (Matthew 25:26).

We can tell by the way Contestant #3 came out with a list of eloquent excuses that he had been rehearsing them for some time; however, excuses do not win the Reality Show of Life—actions do. I can imagine his cutaway interview during the reality show probably going something like this: "When I go before the Host's great white awards throne, I'm going to let the excuses fly because I know He's a very loving and caring Host. I'm sure He will say, 'I understand why you didn't do anything with the skills and talents I gave you. After all, it was a new season of your favorite TV show, and your football team was in the championships! I know how busy you were playing the latest video game, and how *rewarding* it was to conquer the hidden level and defeat the space alien universe. Who could resist reading the brand new novel that your favorite author just released? I don't blame you a bit; I couldn't put it down either! No, really, I understand you didn't know what to do, so you just sat and did nothing.'"

Contestant #3 tried to take advantage of the Host's good nature and completely disregarded the objective, which was to use and increase the talents he was given. However, the Host had to act justly to maintain the integrity and expectations of the game; thus He responded, "You wicked and lazy servant, . . . take the talent from him, and give it to him who has ten talents" (Matthew 25:26, 28, NKJV).

Other Warnings

While God certainly loves us, He is also righteous and just. He cannot accept excuses, as this would diminish the gigantic price that Jesus paid on the cross for us (Romans 3:25–

26). Jesus actually told similar stories in the Bible of not accepting excuses, including the Parable of the Great Supper (Luke 14:15–24) and the Cost of Discipleship (Luke 9:57–62).

Jesus' purpose in telling multiple stories with the same moral means that He's not kidding around about how we conduct ourselves. We've been given one life; there are no do-overs or extra life lines. It's our responsibility to make this life count, and to do this, we should be focusing on the correct things so we can wind up like Contestants #1 and #2.

The Main Thing

I know it can be overwhelmingly profound when we talk about biblical truths, and it can even start our minds racing with a multitude of trivial side questions. However, we can keep it simple by focusing on the main points of the parable:

- We are to discover the talents He left us and increase them.

- Our Master is coming back at an unknown time, and He will ask what we did with the talents He left us.

- Our goal is to hear, "**Well done, thou good and faithful servant**" (Matthew 25:21, KJV).

WELL DONE

Reflection Questions

1. In the Parable of the Talents, which contestant do you most identify with? Why?

2. What excuses have you used to justify not developing the talents you have been given?

Chapter 2—Primary Colors

Now that we have established that our main goal in life is to hear "Well done," we need to take some steps forward in finding and developing our talents. First, I want to share another foundational truth that shaped my identity and gave me the proper perspective in life, and then we will finish this chapter with tangible ways in which you can grow in that truth.

Perspective (Not a Checklist)

With a goal to hear "Well done" from the Lord, a key point we need to consider is whether our lives are going to be more about *doing* rather than *being*. It is so easy to get caught up in the *doing*, wrongly believing that we need to work or perform in a certain way to get to heaven. With this faulty mind-set, we forget to be who we were actually intended to be.

In reality, we do not need to work at all to go to heaven, since Jesus did the work of living a sinless life and paying the ultimate price for sin by being crucified for us. All we have to do is believe in the work He did for us when He died on the cross to pay for our sins and accept Him as our Savior (Romans 10:9–10). This is the most important decision we will make our entire lives. If you haven't done this, now is a great time to take a moment and pray a simple, heartfelt prayer—admitting you have sinned and accepting Jesus as your sinless substitute, which changes your entire eternity.

With our eternity secure, we can live our lives with more purpose and fulfillment.

According to the Parable of the Talents, it appears there are rewards given to believers who increase their abilities and use them wisely. With this in mind, it would be easy for us to get caught up in the "works" mentality and feel like we are hamsters in a wheel, running around and trying to accomplish things for the kingdom in order to earn these rewards. However, if we have the right perspective, then we will use our abilities to lead others to Him out of love and appreciation for the gigantic price Jesus paid for us. Acting out of love and gratitude makes our relationship with God more genuine and our rewards more meaningful.

The One Thing

I accepted Jesus into my heart as an adult through the influence of several business relationships. It was awesome and obviously changed my life for eternity. Then I started attending church, visiting many of them to see which one was a good fit for me. I would listen to these amazing pastors preach, and I was incredibly impacted by their message; yet, some of what they said made me more confused than I was before I became a Christian. These well-meaning pastors would say, "Here is the *one* key to success with God. Here is the *one* thing you need to know out of the Bible." *Okay, I'm ready. Hit me with it.*

One pastor would say, "Without faith, it is impossible to please God." I thought, *Hooray! I have it; that's it! All I have to do is walk in faith.*

Then another preacher would say, "The one thing you need to do is love your neighbor as yourself." *Ok, that seems reasonable, I will add that one too. Now it is walk in faith and love my neighbor.*

Then the next week another would say, "The one thing you need to do is love God with all your heart, mind, and soul." The following week it was obeying the ten commandments. Then it was peace. After that is was grace, and the list continued to grow, with each of them supporting their message by practical wisdom and Scripture.

I know you could probably keep all those things straight, but just when I felt I was figuring it out, the following week a different pastor sent me off in another direction. "Nope not *that* direction, head *this* way." "Now over there!" "Hold it, go this way." Pretty soon I felt like I had a case of whiplash, and my head was a Ping-Pong ball, pelted by the Bible, going in four different directions at the same time. I ended up not knowing what was significant and what I should do. All of this well-meaning and profound advice ultimately caused me to be overwhelmed and confused. Sorry to say, I needed things really basic and simple to understand them.

After several years of hearing all the *"one* things" I should do, I was exhausted and worn out. Soon I got to thinking, *This bites! There must be an easier way.* One day, I had an epiphany, or at least I thought I did. It was simply, *I know Father God made all the colors in the world out of three primary colors. I wonder if He could boil all the dos and don'ts into just three basic things.* That seemed reasonable. I mean, I could probably remember three things. It was the seemingly endless list, added on to each week, where I was having problems. I would think and pray about this occasionally for months, and that led to years with no answer.

WELL DONE

One day I was sitting in my favorite recliner talking with God, and I said, "Well, what about it Father? I really want to know. What are the three primary things that encompass everything I should know?" This was actually the first time in my life I experienced that amazing warmth and goodness cascading down from the top of my head through my body, where I felt completely relaxed and loved. I heard a soft voice inside of me saying, "Mac, there are not three things you need to know, there is only one. The one thing you need to know is how much I love you. If you know how much I love you, all of those other things will be taken care of. Know My love for you and you will have peace, walk in faith, love Me, and you will love others. Everything comes from knowing and receiving My love for you." I cannot tell you the enormity of that moment.

You Are Loved by God

If we don't believe this basic foundational truth of being fully loved by God, nothing else matters. It's the rock-solid foundation upon which everything is built. The primary purpose of your existence is to have a real loving relationship with God, knowing that you are totally loved by Him. Mankind is the most loved and adored of all of God's creation; you were made in His image (Genesis 1:26–30). He loves you more than you can comprehend. All of God's vast, endless love is focused toward you. By receiving this truth, you are able to live your life the way it is intended; acknowledging and receiving God's love makes it easy to love Him back and show His love to others.

Really, if I miss out on a loving relationship with Father God, I'm missing the whole purpose of life. That's why He created us, to have an intimate relationship with Him. God didn't wake up one day and say, "Shazam! I made an earth. I hate to mow lawns. I think I should make a grounds crew to take care of it." No! God created us in His image so we could have a relationship with Him (Genesis 1:27; I Corinthians 1:9).

In order for Contestants #1 and #2 to fulfill the multiplying of their talents, first they had to know that the Reality Show Host loved them no matter what they did with their talents. They weren't afraid of His response because they had accepted His love, and the fruit of that awareness flowed into their actions. These contestants desired to please Him and to do what was right as a response to perfect love.

Being fully and unconditionally loved may sound too easy because it is the opposite of everything we are taught, which is that performance earns love and acceptance. The Parable of the Talents is about rewards for our performance. However, if we do not start from a position of being loved, we will miss out on the joy of serving our Father from a heart of gratitude, rather than obligation.

It can sound so trite to say, "God loves you" or "God loves me." However, the depth of God's love is anything but trite. None of us can fully comprehend the magnitude of His love, and for many of us, there is a mental barrier stopping us from adequately receiving this love. Receiving is a big key; we need to receive God's amazing love. Like any gift, for there to be value, someone has to receive it, or it remains unopened and useless. We will talk about this more, but be open to receiving all that God has for you.

Uncomfortable Love

I know the whole concept of love can seem immensely awkward and impractical in today's fallen world. Many of us grew up in a dysfunctional household, and if we had a father figure in our lives, he may not have adequately reflected the true love that our Father God has for us. I like to joke that if you grew up with two loving parents, you are probably really confused and messed up because that is such a rarity today. Most of us have not experienced being loved unconditionally, simply for who we are.

The world wants to tell us that fulfillment comes from sex, money, drugs, power, possessions, performance, and everywhere else except knowing and accepting that we are fully loved by God. What if we truly understood that we are totally loved, accepted, and even adored by the God of the universe? Would that make our days easier? Would it really matter how big our house is, how expensive our car is, or how attractive we are?

The world judges everything based on looks and worthiness. Are you worthy for the job, position, promotion, relationship, and so on? Are your looks equal to the airbrushed models on TV or the Internet? Father God says that He loves us fully, just as we are, and to show this, He sent His sinless Son to die for us (John 3:16). Out of this awareness, we are then empowered to choose to stop worrying about what label and value the world puts on us, and we become more concerned about fulfilling the purpose of our life.

Sorry—Not Accepted

Would it be in Satan's best interest to convince you that you were being judged all the time and that you were never really accepted and loved by God? "Nope, you didn't quite pray or read your Bible long enough—rejected, you lose." "Oh, bummer, you missed it again." "Whatever you do, it won't be quite good enough and you are unacceptable." "Who could love anybody that looks and acts like you?" "Yes, you did pray for an hour, but your mind was wandering." "Oops, you failed again." So exhausting and discouraging!

Do you remember how we chose teams when we were kids? The two coolest or most athletic kids separated and started choosing teams, and if you were like me, you were always chosen near the last. Often, one of the team captains would say, "You can have Mac. We don't want him on our team." Great news! God stood up and specifically said, "I want you and I pick you first; you are my beloved, the bride of Christ! I choose you and love you unconditionally."

No Zombies

The most important practical step I had to take on my journey to hearing "Well done" was receiving the truth that I am totally loved and accepted just as I am. God values me, regardless of my performance or lack thereof, whether I read the Bible or pray the rest of my life. The interesting thing is when I acknowledged that I was fully loved, I looked forward to reading the Bible and fellowshipping with God, not because I had to, but out of my desire to be with Him. It is natural to move away from areas where you feel condemned and toward areas where you feel loved and accepted.

In order to believe I was loved unconditionally, I had to stop walking in judgment toward myself. I had to renew my mind to accept the truth that God really loved me. This world is all about condemnation, but who wants a relationship with someone if all they do is criticize and find wrong in them? Satan would like to raise an army of zombies, brainwashed by his lies to keep people in condemnation. You have to be aware of this and "take every thought captive" (2 Corinthians 10:5, ESV).

Because of my dysfunctional upbringing, accepting God's love for me was a process that included reading the Bible, finding truths about the Father's love for me, and meditating on them. *God loves me so much that He gave His only Son to die for me* (John 3:16; Romans 5:8). As awkward and corny as it sounds, I had to look in the mirror and tell myself I was chosen and loved by God. I knew if I was uncomfortable looking in the mirror and telling myself how much Father God loved me, I had not succeeded in believing this most basic foundational truth.

As I am writing this, I just took a break, went to the bathroom mirror, looked myself square in the eye, and told myself how much I am passionately loved and adored by God. Wow! I have come a long way from my upbringing of condemnation, and you can too! Why don't you take a quick break, go look in the mirror, and tell yourself God fervently loves you. This is a bold, tangible move to show yourself where you are in the process of realizing and accepting God's incredible love.

Practical Love

There were several things that I did to help saturate my brain in the truth of God's love for me. First Corinthians 13 is called the Love Chapter, so this seemed like a great place to start.

> *Love endures with patience and serenity, love is kind and thoughtful, and is not jealous or envious; love does not brag and is not proud or arrogant. It is not rude; it is not self-seeking, it is not provoked [nor overly sensitive and easily angered]; it does not take into account a wrong endured. It does not rejoice at injustice, but rejoices with the truth [when right and*

truth prevail]. Love bears all things [regardless of what comes], believes all things [looking for the best in each one], hopes all things [remaining steadfast during difficult times], endures all things [without weakening].

Love never fails [it never fades nor ends]. But as for prophecies, they will pass away; as for tongues, they will cease; as for the gift of special knowledge, it will pass away. For we know in part, and we prophesy in part [for our knowledge is fragmentary and incomplete]. But when that which is complete and perfect comes, that which is incomplete and partial will pass away. When I was a child, I talked like a child, I thought like a child, I reasoned like a child; when I became a man, I did away with childish things. For now [in this time of imperfection] we see in a mirror dimly [a blurred reflection, a riddle, an enigma], but then [when the time of perfection comes we will see reality] face to face. Now I know in part [just in fragments], but then I will know fully, just as I have been fully known [by God]. And now there remain: faith [abiding trust in God and His promises], hope [confident expectation of eternal salvation], love [unselfish love for others growing out of God's love for me], these three [the choicest graces]; but the greatest of these is love. (1 Corinthians 13:4–13, AMP)

I took this passage and personalized the words so I could focus on how they applied to God's love for me. For example, verse four would read, "God's love for Mac endures with patience and serenity. God's love toward Mac is kind and thoughtful. God's love toward Mac is not jealous or envious. God's love toward Mac does not brag, and is not proud or arrogant."

This chapter also helped me act in more loving ways toward my wife, family, and others. I made another copy of the same chapter and printed my name wherever I saw the word "love." In this case, verse four would read, "Mac endures with patience and serenity, Mac is kind and thoughtful, and is not jealous or envious. Mac does not brag and is not proud or arrogant," and so on throughout the rest of the chapter.

Being fully loved has nothing to do with performance; it has everything to do with the truth of God's character and our position as His children (Ephesians 2:8–9; Titus 3:5). We love our own children unconditionally, even when they mess up. We understand that they are not perfect, but we still love them because they are our kids. Our Father God loves us so much more, even through all the mistakes we have made. Being loved by God should be our identity, the basic truth of our existence.

Contestant #3 failed to understand the dynamics of the Reality Show and his relationship with the Host. He acted out of fear and laziness because he did not realize how valuable he was to the Host, or how much of an honor it was to be given the talent by Him. When we grasp the concept that we are loved unconditionally, fear and idleness go by the wayside and are replaced by an inner freedom that manifests as an intense desire to follow and please God.

After accepting that God passionately loves us, our next priority on our journey toward hearing "Well done" is to grow our relationship with Him. Having a relationship with God just means we are hanging out with Him, talking to Him, listening to Him, learning more about Him, and seeking guidance about what He would have us do. The closer we draw to God, the more clearly we will see our next steps.

Connection

One of the best tips I was given early in my Christian walk was to consciously include God in all areas of my life. I mean really, He is part of our life all the time anyway, whether we recognize it or not. He is with me as I am writing this book, and He is with you as you are reading it. I am writing this book, receptive to God's guidance for what He would have me include in it. Hopefully, you are actively connecting with God as you are reading to discover what He would have you get out of it. Connecting with God just means looking inside of yourself and seeking God's reflections on what you are reading. Often, His guidance and promptings can feel like a little nudge or tug—confirming certain messages and steps to take or warning us to stay away from harmful messages or actions.

Throughout our day, we can engage with God and ask Him for His thoughts on any situation we encounter. We can seek His wisdom and peace as we are making decisions, and even spend a few minutes in worship and prayer while we are driving the kids to basketball practice, washing the dishes, or mowing the lawn. These are just a few examples, and as we continue to build our relationship with God, we get better at it. The closer we are to Him, the more success we will experience because we are continuously looking to the all-knowing God of the universe for help. As we build this connection and act on what God would have us do, we are developing a sensitivity and awareness to God's leading. The more we focus on God and not ourselves, the closer we get to fulfilling His plan for our lives.

WELL DONE

Bible Reading

Soon after I became a Christian, I heard that reading the Bible was important. I had just one minor problem—my reading level was extremely subpar. I am not sure what the problem was growing up, but when I was a child, my mom would sit with me for hours trying to teach me to read. Since I did not like school, I did not apply myself. I like to jokingly say, "I only missed a few days in school and wouldn't you know it—those are the days they decided to teach reading, writing, spelling, and grammar!" When it came to the Bible, I knew reading it was vital, but I just didn't know how I was going to be able to read and comprehend such an important book. I needed to change my "default thoughts" from what I couldn't do to what I could do.

One thing that really helped me take the next step forward was an audio version of the Bible. I would listen to it in my car and at home. For a long time, I would even go to sleep with the Bible playing in the background. Another thing I did as a new Christian was write down short verses I liked and memorize them. I was not the guy to memorize pages of the Bible, but I would choose key verses that impacted my life.

One of the verses that really encouraged me was Joshua 1:8: "This Book of the Law shall not depart from your mouth, but you shall meditate in it day and night, that you may observe to do according to all that is written in it. For then you will make your way prosperous, and then you will have good success" (NKJV). I really liked the concept of making my way prosperous and having good success. It has a positive ring to it, right? I may not have known *all* that was written in it at that point, but I could figure out what meditate meant, pick a meaningful verse, and focus on it throughout my day. It is about taking one step at a time. God loves the process, and you can thrive in it by finding ways to take a step forward in the process of whom He made you to be.

Meditation

So what does meditate mean? Webster's 1828 English Dictionary states that to meditate is "[t]o dwell on anything in thought; to contemplate; to study; to turn or revolve any subject in the mind."[1] I used to meditate all the time; the only problem was the meditating I did was actually called worrying. When we worry, we continue to meditate or ponder a thought in a negative way. We think of all the possible bad outcomes, and throughout the day we continue to mull them over in our minds. *Oh, my boss said he wanted a meeting with me tomorrow. I wonder what he wants? Maybe they are going to close the company. I know! Maybe he is going to fire me, and then I will lose my income and be homeless. I'll be embarrassed, living on the street with no friends.* Some of us are incredible meditators. We just aren't meditating on the right things. When we allow these possible negative outcomes to take over our thoughts, it can often lead us down the path of making those outcomes a reality.

Let's say we build up this negative scenario in our heads that our boss is going to fire us. How would that affect our attitude toward him? Would we waste company time spewing negative things about him to our coworkers? How would that affect their relationship with the boss and their level of respect for him? Do you see how this could lead to a self-fulfilling prophesy of getting fired? Constantly bombarded with negative newscasts and TV programs, it is easy to see how some of us have nothing but negative thoughts on our minds. Yet we can be so much more prosperous in life if we focus on the positives.

Successful meditation starts by just taking a Bible verse and pondering it from a positive direction. Again, we look at Joshua 1:8. *Wow! The Bible, God's Word, says I can have good success! Okay, I like good success. I'll bet good success means God wants me to be happy and content with Him. That sounds good to me. God also probably wants to help me with my job and my family. This is awesome! I like thinking about these powerful thoughts day and night. Thank you, God! Your Word is truth. Please reveal more of Your promises to me.*

Prayer and Praise

Another way of connecting with God is to pray. When I became a Christian, I heard I was supposed to pray, but for me that sounded so stuffy and religious. When I was taught as a kid to pray, I had to fold my hands just right, sit still (as if that was going to happen), shut my eyes, bow my head, and say the perfect words in King James English with a certain reverent tone. For many people, prayer is a big mystical thing with a hundred rules, and if you do not do it just right, God will not hear you. Can you say, baloney?

The truth is God just wants me connected to Him, and praise and prayer are just ways we can converse with Him. Just because you cannot see Him doesn't mean He's not listening. Uttering "thee" and "thou" and "hallowed" in medieval English blended with our best radio announcer voice is not going to get His attention any faster than just talking to Him like you would your best friend.

Praise gets us in a positive mind-set, builds our faith, and sets good things in motion (Colossians 2:6–7; Acts 16:22–

26). Praise is just saying things about God that are true. I don't think God needs our praise to boost His self-image. I think when I spend time praising and acknowledging God's greatness, it helps me better understand who He is and all that He has done for me. When I focus on the amazing qualities of God, it changes my perspective toward Him. *Father, you are so loving and kind. I praise you for sending Jesus to live a sinless life and for taking my punishment on the cross, while He was innocent. I praise you for sending your Holy Spirit as a Helper and Counselor.* Just writing these things and saying them makes me feel better inside, and it focuses my thoughts to those truths.

As we praise God, it allows us to also accept ourselves. People who have low self-esteem often have a difficult time giving compliments to others, or they may do it out of envy and jealousy. Accepting God's love for us is to say, "I am loved; therefore, I can also give love."

A great benefit of prayer is finding out what God wants us to do. When I began dating my wife, Dianne, I prayed to God and asked for a word or a sign from Him, letting me know if and when I should marry her. I remember telling our pre-marriage counselor that because I had been in so many bad relationships in the past, I would not marry Dianne unless God spoke to me. He said, "Mac, that's crazy! God doesn't always speak to people about this stuff." I said, "Listen, God knows what I have been through with bad relationships, so read my lips: I'm not marrying Dianne unless God speaks to me. Period. End of conversation."

I cared about Dianne, but I literally gave it all to God with no preconception of what I wanted. A couple of months later, I was driving down a main street of our city and I heard an internal voice say, "Okay, you can marry Dianne now." I went and proposed to her, and shortly afterward we were married. Even through the bumpy times of our marriage, I have had complete peace that we were supposed to be together.

On a side note, some people could use this example and say, "Okay, that gives me an excuse to get out of my marriage since God never spoke to me." Not so fast my friend. I have seen the most miserable couples succeed in marriage when they gave their marriage to God. I have also seen the most perfect couples who had been brought together by God split when they failed to keep God at the center of their marriage. I know this might not be popular, but an infinite God can change any situation, even a struggling marriage. Whoever we are married to is who we should be married to, and any marriage can be repaired if we pray and follow God's Word.

Prayer and God's Provision

We read that God answers prayer; however, there is so much more I have to learn about its power. When I sit back and reflect on my career and the things in my life, I have to give God the credit. In prayer, God shows me my next steps, and with each step I take, a new door opens and connects me with His blessings.

Two years before I changed professions, I saw a picture in my mind of the work I would be doing and even the office where I would be working. As I look around today, I know many of my possessions are from God, including my mountain bike which was sold to me below the wholesale price. I also just happened to walk into the close-out area of the furniture store and got the desk I am currently working at for half price. If you look, it is amazing how often you see God's hand in multiple areas of your life. Although these are some of the less important tangible things that He provides for us, there is also a gigantic list of intangibles, including a happier marriage, peace, and contentment. How do you put a price on those things?

As we accept that God loves us unconditionally and we connect to Him through reading our Bible, giving Him praise, and praying, we are building a genuine relationship with Him. If we are focusing on strengthening our relationship with God, the devil's influence is minimized, and we become stronger for the kingdom of God.

WELL DONE

Reflection Questions

1. Why do you serve God? Are you more motivated by love, fear, or some other emotion?

2. Is accepting God's unconditional love for you uncomfortable? If so, in what ways do you try to earn God's love?

3. How do you include God in your everyday life?

4. What are some "default thoughts" that are hindering your relationship with God?

5. What is one of your favorite verses? Write it down and meditate on it this week.

Chapter 3—Traps

As a business and organizational coach, leaders want me to warn them about possible problems or traps I see coming down the road. I want to do the same for you. Satan would love nothing more than to destroy the relationship that we have with God, but that's not such an easy feat when we have a strong connection with the Father. So, being the great deceiver, the devil sets obstacles or traps to get us off track and lose focus of finding our purpose and fulfilling our God-given destiny—ultimately preventing us from hearing "Well done." We need to become aware of these traps in order to avoid them.

Confusion

Satan wants us to be confused so we will do nothing. For instance, bad things happen because of Satan, but he wants us to think otherwise. Just think of all the bad things that happen in the world. Would a loving God do all those bad things to the world and the children He created? The real truth is bad things happen in the world for one reason: Satan is here (John 12:31; 2 Corinthians 4:4). If there were no Satan and no sin, we would live in a perfect world.

Once again, the devil wants to trick us into believing that somehow God is doing bad things to us instead of the great deceiver, himself. If he can get us to accept his lies, he will succeed in creating doubt and getting us to do nothing positive with our lives—a big win for him. Confusion is a common trap that can take our focus off of the truth of God's amazing love for us, so we must avoid it by going to God in prayer and searching His Word for revelation and understanding.

What Trap?

An interesting trap that Satan can get us into is one of not believing we are in a trap at all. Do any of these thoughts sound familiar? *All of these bad things you are experiencing are normal. God isn't real, so you can't count on Him to connect with you. Your life of abuse is just typical. There is nothing really wrong with the way you are living. If you really use your imagination, maybe you won't see it as a metal trap you're caught in, or the emotional cage in which you exist. Just see the trap as normal, as part of who you are. After all, it is really protecting you from not living a fuller life with more risks, so maybe it is an advantage and not a trap after all.*

Satan wants us to believe the trap we are in is normal, so we will not figure out Jesus has already freed us from Satan's trap and we can walk in newness of life.

Blaming Others

One of the most common traps that Satan uses is blaming others for our actions. We see this all the way back in the Garden of Eden when Adam blamed Eve for giving him the forbidden fruit, and in turn, Eve blamed the serpent for deceiving her (Genesis 3:12–13). If God did not accept them passing blame back then, He will not accept us doing that today. In the Parable of the Talents, we are shown that at the end of time on this earth, each of us is responsible for and will be rewarded based on what we have done or have failed to do with our lives. The only one you have to answer for is you—not your pastor, not your spouse, not what you believed out of your science book, or what your parrot Fritzy told you. It's all going to be about what you did with what He gave you.

Strongholds

"But Mac, an event happened when I was a child that was devastating. I had no control over it; therefore, I *am* a victim of circumstances and am not responsible for my actions." I understand, and chances are I would wholly agree that what happened to you was horrible and outside of your control. Life can be hard, brutal, and completely unfair. The question is are you going to let it hold you back, like Contestant #3 when he only got one talent, or will you grow from it?

The issue is not what occurs in our lives but how we interpret and respond to those events. Eventually, bad things happen to us all. We live in a fallen world, and that is just the way it is. We can allow those terrible experiences to wreck our lives, or we can look to God for help to get us through these situations and on to more positive results. The decision is ultimately ours. Let me give you a couple of examples.

Have you ever heard someone retell a hurtful event or an offense that happened many years ago? Did he retell it like, "Oh, this is the first time I ever thought about how they treated me so badly ten years ago," or did it seem like it was fresh in his mind, as if it happened a few hours ago? How many times do you think he has replayed the event in his head, reliving every detail and maybe even exaggerating the event in his mental rerun over many years? Perhaps ten, twenty, probably more like hundreds or even thousands of times that he has meditated on and repeated these thoughts.

WELL DONE

Many of those who have been hurt think the same thoughts continually, day in and day out. While they are highly consistent in their meditation, they are focusing on the wrong things. If we have thought about or relived the same event thousands of times in a negative way, do you think you could call that a stronghold in your mind? The problem is that the things we continually meditate on shape who we are and what we become.

I ran into a high school classmate some time back who had a very hard time with alcohol. She lost her marriage, numerous jobs, and her children, and has been incarcerated, all because of alcohol abuse. While talking with her, she indicated that the reason for her trouble was that her dad died on her thirteenth birthday. I absolutely agree that this was a tragic event at a formative time of her life. My heart truly goes out to her. However, because she has replayed this event in her mind from a negative perspective, literally thousands and thousands of times, not only did she reap terrible consequences, so did her children. She lost everything that was important to her, and her kids lost their mom because of how she chose to think about the death of her father.

Please understand that I am not minimizing what happened to her; it was terrible! I am questioning how she was allowing it to control her life. We have all heard stories of people with the same or worse tragedies in their past, and they have replayed the event in their brain as a reason to succeed, not as a justification for failure. We have all had heartbreaking experiences in our lives. Dianne and I had a daughter killed in a car crash, our son went to prison, and we have gone through huge financial collapses. Yes, these events were terrible, but it was up to us to decide how we would relate to them. Would we use them as a reason to give up and fail, or would we allow God to use those trials in our lives to help us minister to others?

As part of leading ourselves, it is up to us to guard our hearts and take control of our thought life. I encourage you to read the following verses on this topic and take them to heart: Proverbs 4:23, 2 Corinthians 10:3–5, and Philippians 4:8. Will we allow God to make something good out of the messes of our lives? He can and will if we let Him (Romans 8:28).

I Can't

Focusing on what we can't do is definitely a trap (I talk more about this subject later on in the book). If we conclude that our lives and relationship with God could be better, that is a wonderful, positive first step toward success. Unfortunately, if we don't believe we can obtain this goal, we haven't advanced very far. I don't want to belittle people's real-life problems, but some people I listen to are intent on continually telling me (and themselves) that their situation is hopeless and they can't ever find an answer. I hear them make statements like, "I can't!" "There's just nothing I can do." "I don't know what to do." "I don't see anything I can do." "There is no answer," and on and on. When I'm talking with these people, it's like I'm playing a mental game of checkers: whatever positive encouraging suggestion I give, they have already planned six comments ahead. It's like they are thinking, *If he gives me this suggestion of something good, I will respond with "That won't work and here is the reason…"* Pretty soon, I'm exhausted. It's a game that no one wins.

I have run into this many times in work environments. People get stuck on a problem and all they can think about is, *I can't figure this out. I don't know.* Let me ask you a serious question. If we repeat over and over, *I don't know* and *I can't figure it out* in our amazing, priceless minds God blessed us with, is it possible this is actually blocking our mind from coming up with an answer? We need to always believe God has answers for us, and from my experience, if we are coming from a position of adamant belief that there is an answer or solution, it always appears.

I use the following tool to help people work through this "can't" mentality. I say, "What if I paid you $100,000 at the end of the month as an incentive to figure out an answer, but you couldn't use the $100,000 toward the answer? Could you come up with some steps to move forward?" When I'm stuck in this mental trap, I need to create some baby steps of things I could do to get me moving. Once I take a step, practically no matter how small it is, it helps me move forward to the next step, and I keep asking myself the same question, *OK, Mac what could you do now?*

If Only

During some part of our lives, most of us have caught a case of the "if onlys"—one of the devil's favorite traps. "**If only** I was out of school." "**If only** I didn't have to go to school." "**If only** I had my degree from college." "**If only** I was married." "**If only** I wasn't married." "**If only** I would have married someone else." "**If only** they hadn't married someone else." "**If only** I had a different job." "**If only** I won the lottery." "**If only**..." The list is endless because if we are in this trap, nothing is quite right for us to get moving. There is always a reason why we can't achieve success in our lives.

This is the only life we get, so no matter what cards we were dealt from life's deck, we better be ready to play them to the fullest. Whatever positions we are in, let's accept it and prayerfully move forward. I hear people say, "I believe it's God will for me to go back to school, but I'm married." Long awkward pause. Okay, I assume when God told you to go back to school, He knew your situation and had resources for you. Otherwise, why did He tell you that? Oh, you didn't think he knew you were married and had kids? Really, I think God may be a little smarter than we give Him credit.

Blankieville

Aren't little kids so cute when they pull a blanket over their heads and think they are invisible? We say, "Where did Cindy go? I don't know—where is she?" It's fun to play this game with a one-year-old child. However, it seems a little awkward when we as adults are still playing the game of pulling our imaginary blankie over our heads and telling ourselves, "I'm sure God doesn't see or care what I'm doing. My imaginary blankie will shield me from His sight." It just doesn't seem quite as cute when adults play the "God can't see me" game. Not to keep beating up on Adam and Eve, because they were human like you and me, but they played a little imaginary game of hide and seek from God using a blankie of leaves to cover their nakedness after they ate the forbidden fruit (Genesis 3:6–13). They were essentially saying, "With our leaf blankies, we hoped you wouldn't see us."

Like Adam and Eve, we somehow deceive ourselves into thinking that how we live our lives is hidden from the sight of an all-knowing God. God saw their decision in the Garden of Eden, and all of mankind ultimately felt the consequences. I believe that our decisions also have ramifications, maybe not for all of mankind, but they have substantial implications for our own lives, our descendants' lives, and our eternity.

Another Season of Guilt Reruns

Satan would love to get some of us to fall into his trap of living in guilt and condemnation over how we have lived our lives up to this point. Once again, this is unprofitable. Personally, I made a total mess of my early years with partying, drugs, alcohol abuse, illicit relationships, and the list goes on and on. The only thing I could do was humbly ask an all-loving God for forgiveness, receive His amazing love, mercy, and grace, and move forward. God didn't send Jesus to condemn us but to save us (John 3:17).

If I spend my time rehashing the seemingly endless list of dumb decisions I made, I'm just adding one more bad choice to the pile instead of looking ahead and using the rest of my earthly time in a more productive manner for the kingdom of God. Replaying another season of how bad we have messed up our lives will not do anything to make the present season more successful. Cancel your subscription now to the "Self-Guilt and Condemnation Show" playing on your History channel.

The same thing applies to those who accept God's love later on in life. Once you understand what the true focus of your time should be, you need to move in that new direction of serving God without a moment's hesitation. As I tell my kids, "There's no time like the present. We're burning daylight, so let's get to work!" We may not know how much time we have left on this earth, but we can live out our days in a more positive way, rather than doing nothing or living in regret.

Wasted Time

Doing nothing, like Contestant #3, is a huge trap Satan uses to diminish our impact for the kingdom of God. I can remember when I first became sensitive to time. I would come home after a big day at work and kick back on the couch. I would sit there all night and stare at the TV, like I was trying to hone my skills for the next zombie movie tryouts. The same thing happened when I was at the computer. I would play games, read social media, and look at negative news for hours on end. What it boiled down to was whether I was watching TV or looking at the computer, I was spending my life watching other people live their lives instead of turning off the electronics and living life myself. I can remember even at a young age thinking, *Mac, you spent all day watching TV or playing video games when you could have been out playing and living life.* As an adult, I thought the same thing: *Why am I wasting my whole life on meaningless things?* Ultimately all the things I was doing had zero significance, except to waste the most valuable thing I have, which are the minutes and hours that comprise my very life existence until Jesus comes back.

We can spend our time reading a novel, zoning out, or watching TV, but most of us do not realize that these activities are using up the very limited supply of time that has been entrusted to us. While it takes little effort to waste time, it takes great effort to use time properly. We can only spend each moment one time, and eventually most people look up and realize that we really do not have much time on this earth. Maybe we look in the mirror and think, *I didn't see those wrinkles before*, or *It looks like I'm getting more gray hair*, or even *It's taking me longer to get out of bed these days*. We are hit with the reality of our mortality. Yet we can choose to look at it in a strategic way, investing our limited time into things that can make a positive impact. We can decide to purposely love people and invest our talents in those who can keep on loving and positively influencing others after we are gone. Doing this will make us agents of change, leaving a lasting legacy that continues after we physically pass on from this earth.

Parked Cars

Sir Isaac Newton's first Law of Motion states, "Every object will remain at rest or in uniform motion in a straight line unless compelled to change its state by the action of an external force." Sometimes we can get caught up in the devil's trap of uncertainty concerning God's will for our lives, and it winds up paralyzing us from doing anything constructive for the Lord. I learned to take some action, even if it might be wrong. A pastor friend of mine is fond of saying, "It's tough to steer a parked car." So if you're currently motionless, I would encourage you to get moving and do something so you can be directed.

I used to be a procrastinator. I would spend all of my time focusing on what I didn't know how to do, which caused me to do absolutely nothing. Finally, I got upset with myself. *Mac, you are always looking at all the things that you can't do or don't know how to do. Is there anything you can do?*

I kept questioning myself over and over, looking for what I could do, and it usually boiled down to taking some baby steps to get me moving forward. For instance, perhaps I believe I am supposed to write a book, but I think I can't write an entire book. *Cool, Mac. Could you take a class on writing? Could you sharpen your pencil? Could you turn on the computer or maybe even open the Word document?*

It is like dieting. Most people can't fathom losing 100 pounds; that's crazy! However, we could start by figuring out what we can do, like finding where we stashed our walking shoes and then going for a stroll around the block, or maybe tossing out the junk food. If we just keep thinking about the next little steps we can take, instead of stopping all the motion by looking at what we can't do, God will reveal His wonderful plan for our lives and continue to direct our path.

Dishonoring Authority

We can stunt the good work that God is doing in our lives by falling into the trap of dishonoring those in positions of authority. To say I had a problem with authority growing up is a colossal understatement. The teacher would say, "Class, we are going to read Mark Twain," and I would tell myself, *Mac, make a note of that. Never read Mark Twain as long as you live.* The teacher would say, "Class, highlight this sentence in your book so you can remember it." I complied . . . with a solid black marker so I would never see the words again.

There is a distinct reason why I got in so much trouble, was kicked out of school multiple times, and ultimately left school and home at age sixteen. I worked on my own most of my adult life because I did not like to submit to authority and have people telling me what to do. After thirty-five years of running and developing my own companies, I went to work for a church with—and you're not going to believe this—a boss. I had matured enough to know that submitting to authority was a godly attribute and could help both the organization and me.

Submission to authority is a God-honoring trait (I Peter 5:5–6). My ability to submit and follow leadership sends a gigantic message to the whole organization that this is the proper thing to do. Our whole team honors our leaders, and it creates a positive, healthy workforce. It is my experience, as well as a biblical principle, that God will not honor people who are too prideful to honor and submit to authority.

Disunity

Refusing to submit to authority can often lead to spreading discord—especially within the church. Spreading discord is one of the most damaging traps; in fact, it is actually one of the seven abominations or things that God hates (Proverbs 6:16–19).

It doesn't take a genius to find reasons to disagree with other people and their decisions. As wild as it seems, sometimes I don't even agree with myself after looking back and reflecting on my previous decisions. There are many different Christian perspectives, but Paul wrote to the churches to walk in unity with other believers (I Corinthians 1:10; Romans 15:5–6; Ephesians 4:1–6). Unity means that we are looking for and finding things on which we can agree.

Instead of focusing on the fact that we, as Christians, believe Jesus is the Son of God and He died to forgive our sins, we often get caught up in the minutia that has nothing to do with bringing people to Christ. We argue over the difference in the recipe for our communion wafers, the color of our carpet, if the seats should be padded, the type of music, and whether or not it's okay to raise our hands in worship.

You may say, "Mac, those issues are foolish! Our church split up for important, fundamental reasons." Are the reasons significant enough to fall into one of the seven things that God hates? Don't get me wrong; there are theological issues that are worth debating, but there is one overarching reason we should look to be united, and that is because Jesus told us to "love one another: just as I have loved you, you also are to love one another. By this all people will know that you are my disciples" (John 13:34–35, ESV). Loving each other and having unity exemplifies how Jesus loves the world.

I'm not saying we can or will be united in every single area of belief; none of us are going to have it totally figured out this side of heaven. I'm saying that we were told to set a good example of love and unity, and we should actively seek ways to come together, avoid the devil's traps, and accomplish the things for which God put us on earth to do—so we can hear those two words, "Well done."

WELL DONE

Reflection Questions

1. What traps have you fallen into that have kept you from developing a deeper relationship with God?

2. Identify three "time wasters" in your life that are diminishing your impact for the kingdom of God.

3. What are three small steps you could take within the next week to help you fulfill something God has called you to do?

4. What are a few things you can do to foster unity with other believers?

Chapter 4—Warning

I spoke recently at a large church and asked one of my favorite questions, "How many of you know someone who has gotten offended and quit the church?" It appeared that every hand went up. My follow-up question was, "Out of all the people who got offended and quit going to church, how many of them are better off now?" I didn't see a single hand raised. While I'm sure some people could give me a decent argument for why they are better off not going to church, the Bible says God wants His followers to come together in unity to encourage each other and be in His presence (Hebrews 10:24–25; Matthew 18:20).

After conducting an officially unofficial survey of why people quit going to church, it appears the number-one reason people leave the church is that they get offended. These offended people may or may not tell you the truth as to why they left. Sometimes they use ambiguous words to describe their actions, but it generally comes down to a personal offense. Usually after I talk with these people for a while, they reveal why they really left. "That pastor made me mad," or "That person took my parking place, didn't say hi to me, they are all a bunch of hypocrites, I can't get over it, and I'm out of here!" I heard this so many times that I decided I would do a little biblical investigation on the subject of offense.

Skandalon

The Bible was primarily written in Hebrew or Greek, mainly Hebrew in the Old Testament and Greek in the New Testament. Sometimes by looking at the original translation of words, we get a clearer understanding of what the author was trying to convey. In the New Testament, the Greek word for offense is *skandalon*.

Skandalon: the movable stick or trigger of a trap; a trap, snare; any impediment placed in the way and causing one to stumble or fall; any person or thing by which one is (entrapped) drawn into error or sin.[2]

If offense can be a method of entrapment, we can be caught by our own devices, including our own thinking!

Wow! For me this was a powerful revelation. Satan is trying to get us offended at each other in order to catch us in his gigantic trap of causing disunity among the believers so we won't be as effective for the kingdom of God. He doesn't care who offends us—the guy driving carelessly down the road, our spouse, our boss, our pastor—as long as we are offended by someone, take his bait, and get caught up in his trap.

Motive

It is easy to get offended when we assume the motivation for someone's actions. You know how it works. Someone behaves in a certain way that seems rude, unloving, or otherwise distasteful toward us. Instead of just observing the behavior, we assume we know the thoughts that motivated those actions, and we judge it as offensive. This has happened to me so many times over the years, and I am continually embarrassed at how quickly I can jump to conclusions.

MAC MAYER

For instance, as I was talking with someone on the phone the other day, the person's voice got louder and more intense. Suddenly, the phone went dead. I made all sorts of negative assumptions about what had happened. My imagination ran wild with thoughts about what he was thinking, and how discourteous he was to me before he so rudely hung up. When I spoke with him later, he said, "Sorry I was so loud on the phone, but I was in the lobby of a hotel and a large group of people came through. I had to yell to be able to continue our conversation. I didn't think about it, but as I stepped onto the elevator and the door closed, I lost my cell signal." When I found out what really happened, I was thoroughly embarrassed because for the twenty-four hours after our interrupted phone conversation, I had considered him every barnyard animal and lower life form that ever existed.

What I learned from that experience is that I can never assign a motivation to someone's behavior. All I know for sure is that he was speaking loudly and we got disconnected. I have no evidence of anything else. This happens every day with people misinterpreting e-mails, texts, and conversations. This also happens in churches. "My Bible study leader walked past me in the hall and didn't say hi to me. I guess she doesn't like me." "The pastor preached that sermon because he thinks I'm a pervert." "The children's director didn't give my kids a big part in the Christmas play. I knew she had it out for them!" The truth is I cannot really tell what a person is thinking, no matter what their actions, words, or body language seem to indicate. The moral of the story is let's not assign a motivation to others' behaviors, because most likely we will be wrong and fall into the trap of offense.

WELL DONE

If I'm Offended, I'm Wrong

Jesus commanded that if we have something against our brother, we are to go to him, talk it over, and resolve it (Matthew 18:15–17). I can't do anything about the other person; I can only do something about me. If I'm offended, unforgiving, carrying a grudge, and not walking in peace, the bottom line is I'm wrong. I need to forgive the other person, or even myself, get over it, and move on, or I will stay in Satan's *skandalon* trap and it could ruin my life.

We have all had bad things happen to us. God's love and mercy are the only things that have helped me through these difficult times. *Father, you have forgiven me for so much; I gladly forgive them and not only that, I bless them.* I can tell if I'm still offended if I'm still thinking bitter thoughts. It doesn't matter what the other person did or didn't do; I need to forgive them. How am I supposed to hear, "Well done. Enter into the joy of the Lord," when I am far from joyful, carrying bitterness and holding grudges? In my own struggles with unforgiveness, I came up with a way to overcome this obstacle.

When people who had wronged me came to mind, instead of mentally blasting them, I learned to pray, *Father, please forgive them*, and *Father, I pray that you would just shower them with love and blessing today.* The more I was bitter, the more I knew I had to increase speaking blessings over them to free myself from the offense trap. My mind would scream, *But I don't want to bless them!* I was like a captured animal writhing in a trap of offense. I would stay up all night tossing and turning; I couldn't function normally because I was trapped by my thoughts. I was continually recounting all the bad that had been done to me.

If I'm offended, hurt, unforgiving, or holding on to a grudge, I'm wrong. I need to change and continually forgive and bless the people who have offended me until I have peace and am released from Satan's trap.

Fill the Container

If I put red food coloring in a glass of water, it will stay red until I flush it out. It won't do me any good to curse at the colored water or add more red to it. The only thing that will bring change is to flood the glass with fresh, clean water. When it comes to areas of hurt or offense, this is what I have to do to my mind. I have to flood it with fresh, clean thoughts of love and forgiveness, and not add more red, hateful thoughts to it. I can do this by meditating on Scriptures about God's amazing love for me, listening to uplifting music, praying, and just spending time in His presence.

My goal is to mature to the point that I cannot be offended, no matter what people do or say to me. Whether someone cuts me off midway through my sentence or cuts me off on the freeway, my goal is to live with a flexible outlook and an "it's okay" attitude. (By the way, this goes completely against my personality.) When I do this, I'm happier no matter what those around me are doing.

It's a challenge for me to take on the characteristic of being unable to be offended; however, I want to be continually filled with love so I am unable to receive any offense. If someone comes up to me and says, "You are the most worthless person on the face of the earth!" I can say, "Wow, I really appreciate you taking time out of your busy day to share that with me." I do need to analyze what they say to see if I can grow from it, but after that I'm moving past it. They could be having a bad day, confusing me with someone else, or perhaps they totally have the wrong impression of my situation or of me. My goal is to be the best I can be, but I understand I can't please everyone. There is only One I need to please in this life, and my goal is to hear, "Well done" from Him.

The Love Default

Jesus, the Son of God, came to this earth as a man and went through the ultimate offense of dying a painful and humiliating death for our sins. He lived a sinless life, was whipped and then crucified for the sins of the entire world, and continued to walk in love. On the cross, Jesus prayed, "Father, forgive them, for they do not know what they do" (Luke 23:34, NKJV). Throughout His life, no matter what injustices He faced, He still walked in love. So, until we surpass that, I guess we should follow Jesus' model and walk in forgiveness and love in everything.

In life, it seems like we always run into situations with people that we don't know how to handle. A great way to work our way through any circumstance and avoid the trap of offense is to default to love. When I don't know how to respond to a tough situation with my wife or others, it's good if I ask the question, *What would love do in this situation?* I revert back to the Love Chapter (1 Corinthians 13) where I inserted my name every time I saw the word "love." Remember? Now, you try it.

> *[Your name] is not rude; [Your name] is not self-seeking, [Your name] is not provoked [nor overly sensitive and easily angered]; [Your name] does not take into account a wrong endured. [Your name] does not rejoice at injustice, but rejoices with the truth [when right and truth prevail]. [Your name] bears all things*

[regardless of what comes], believes all things [looking for the best in each one], hopes all things [remaining steadfast during difficult times], endures all things [without weakening]. (1 Corinthians 13:5–7, AMP, additions mine)

These principles become a guide to how we should respond with each situation we face. What would love do? Would love respond at all? What tone of voice would love use? What body language would love use?

Love doesn't mean you need to be a doormat and participate in or put up with other people's garbage. If I'm going to respond in love, I have to love myself and love others. Walking in love doesn't mean that everyone gets their way and the answer is always yes. Walking in love can mean having boundaries and saying no. As you can see from the life of Jesus, sometimes He was very gentle and caring in His response (John 8:11; Luke 23:34). Other times He was very strong and even aggressive (Matthew 21:12–13). What would love do in our daily situations with our spouses, our children, friends, neighbors, and coworkers?

We should also show love in challenging family, church, or business scenarios. Even in professional settings, it's still always beneficial to ask, "What would love do?" When I'm coaching organizations, I normally ask, "What would love do in this situation?" Acting in love might mean I need to terminate an employee. "Okay, if I had to fire someone, how would I do it if I were walking in love?" Most of the books I have read give scenarios and say, "Handle this problem in this way." However, every situation has a unique set of factors, and they are never exactly the same.

WELL DONE

Acting in love seems to be the great equalizer that balances out needs for compassion and consequences and helps me respond in the most appropriate way, while considering all unique parameters of the situation. Every person and situation we deal with is different. When I am uncertain about how love would respond, I can always go back to 1 Corinthians 13, pray, and seek God's wisdom for answers. Ultimately, if I answer from a mature, loving position, God will honor this response because "Love covers a multitude of sins" (1 Peter 4:8, ESV).

Reflection Questions

1. Has making an assumption about someone else's motivations ever gotten you into trouble? If so, how did you resolve the situation?

2. Are you carrying around offense? What are some steps you can take toward forgiveness?

3. Are you facing any potential difficult or tense situations with people in your life right now? How could you approach the problem from a position of love?

Chapter 5—The Secret to Life

The 1991 American Western comedy film, *City Slickers*, is about three middle-aged men looking for the answers to life. There is a pivotal moment when riding side by side on horseback, wannabe cowboy, Mitch Robbins (Billy Crystal) is talking with the sage cowboy, Curly (Jack Palance), and the conversation transitions into the secret of life. Weathered, leather-faced Curly looks at Mitch and rhetorically asks, "Do you know what the secret of life is? . . . One thing. Just one thing. You stick to that and the rest don't mean [anything]." Mitch follows up with, "But, what is the 'one thing'?" Curly's profound but basic answer is, "That's what *you* have to find out."[3]

Well, we are way ahead of the guys in the movie because we already know that the "one thing" is accepting Jesus' love for us. However, this leads to the more specific follow-up question. Beyond accepting His love and avoiding traps, what do we do with our lives to hear, "Well done?"

Discover Your Purpose

In order to find out what we should *do*, we need to find out who we were made to *be*. This sounds so simple, and I believe some of us have actually made it harder than it needs to be. Let's look at automobile designs. How can we tell an automobile designer's intended use of a vehicle? Can't we look at the end product and see how it can be used most effectively?

There are muscle cars with big, loud engines that get four miles to the gallon and have three inches of ground clearance. Common sense tells us that these would not be the most practical cars to take off-road, mudding in the desert. There are four-wheel-drive trucks with big tires and two feet of clearance that probably would not be competitive against race cars at a NASCAR track, but they can take you on a great hunting trip. I don't know about you, but I'd feel so much more comfortable living, sleeping, eating, and watching movies in a motor home rather than in a two-door compact car! Likewise, we don't see fish successful at swinging from trees or dogs good at building dams. We see the differences among cars, homes, plants, animals, and so forth, and we can determine what they were created to do. Even when all of creation around us has a completely obvious blueprint, how many of us have looked at ourselves and said we have absolutely no idea what we were designed to do? Puzzling.

If we are going to hear "Well done," we must figure out what God made us to do. It's great to say, "Yes, God has a plan for your life," but the next thing that needs to happen is to figure out that plan. God has created us all with unique gifts and talents that we can use in our vocation, family life, within our church body—everywhere we go. Because our career/vocation impacts so much of our lives and takes so much of our time, let's discuss this area first.

Honey, You Can Do Anything

I have had the pleasure of speaking with a multitude of high school teens, and one of the most common questions society asks them is, "What are you going to do with your future?" This question can be overwhelming and confusing to teens and sometimes to adults as well. The first thing I want them to do is relax and really believe that God loves them and He wants them to find and fulfill the purpose He has for their lives. The next thing I do is start asking them questions.

There are literally thousands of things that we are not interested in or gifted to do. This greatly reduces the number of possibilities. I ask questions of the teens such as, "What do you think about being a doctor?" Some respond, "I hate blood, I don't like science, and I barely passed Math 101." With one question, we may have wiped out hundreds of jobs in a variety of industries. When we start asking these kinds of questions, we quickly discover a multitude of careers in which we have little interest, or we are just not mentally equipped to do. This can actually be empowering when we realize all of the occupations we *aren't* supposed to pursue.

Many teens have been told the lie that they can succeed in anything they choose, if they just make up their minds to do it. While I love the intent of those words that are meant to be encouraging and inspiring, this just isn't correct. If they're doing something they're not designed to do, first off, they will likely be miserable, and second, they will experience less success. It would be good if we could start weeding out all of the nearly impossible things in which we could really never succeed.

The reality is God has specifically made each one of us with certain characteristics, and it is up to us to discover what these traits are and how they can be utilized. Before we get to that, let my formative years in education be a lesson in what NOT to do when seeking to develop your strengths.

WELL DONE

Behind the Door

Growing up, I occasionally heard the comment, "Mac, you must have been behind the door when God was giving out brains." The not-so-uplifting inference was I had missed out on getting any brains. For years, I was looking at what I couldn't do.

I remember the very first day I walked into Mr. Nelson's (no relation to Mrs. Nelson, my eighth grade English teacher; more on her later) seventh-grade drafting class. Mr. Nelson started off by asking, "Is there a Mac Mayer in this class?" I nervously raised my hand to half-mast. He then boldly proclaimed, "I understand you can't draw a straight line for one inch with a ruler." *Okay, welcome to drafting class.* I'm glad the rumors of my acclaimed drawing and mechanical capabilities had gotten to the class long before I ever showed up. What a great introduction and confidence builder. What's even worse was this statement was pretty close to accurate. While it may not have been the best solution, the only way I ultimately passed drafting class was to pay my classmates to do my projects.

This scenario was pretty typical. I was continually reminded my whole life of the things I couldn't do. "Mac, you can't sit still." "You can't focus." "You don't seem to be able to read." "Why can't you learn grammar and basic writing skills?" "Why can't you do wood shop, work on a car, or understand about construction and mechanical things?" People associated so many letters of the alphabet with my name, I thought for sure I was supposed to be a doctor. "Mac is ADHD-LMNOP." It seemed like everyone just reinforced what I couldn't do. It didn't help that my two older sisters were straight-A students, which I was kindly reminded of on a regular basis.

I can remember when I was in eighth-grade English class and Mrs. Nelson said, "You better learn how to read, write, and spell because someday you're going to want to get a job and no one will hire you if you don't know it." I shot back, "I don't need to learn this junk because when I get older, I will hire people who know how to read, write, and spell." This answer seemed totally logical in my adolescent mind; however, soon after that, while I was sitting in the principal's office for the forty-fifth time, I received the subtle revelation that some things are so obvious they are better left unsaid.

In school, if you are bad at math, what do they say? "You need to stay after school and spend more time on your math; maybe you need to take extra math classes." This is exactly what happened to me. "Mac, you are very bad in all these areas, so our plan is for you to stay after school and devote all of your energy to them." This is where I first learned the concept of an eternal hell. They wanted me to focus all of my energy on developing my weaknesses, and they indicated that there was an infinite array of them.

In real life, this is a foolish waste of time and talent. I guess since I'm pathetic at music and mechanical things, I should stop what I'm doing and devote my life to opera and car repair. Seriously, in real life, who does that? I'm not going to waste my life trying to make a living at or excelling in areas where I have absolutely no natural ability and detest doing.

Anybody Can Do That

Rather than focusing all of our energies on things we're not good at doing, we need to reflect on how God made us. We use terms like "natural ability" or "naturally gifted" when talking about the traits with which we are born; however, I believe they have a spiritual origin. I hear people say,

"The abilities I was born with are natural gifts; they aren't spiritual." Wrong-o. We call them natural because we were born with them, but our Spiritual Father gave all of our natural gifts to us. Anything we can do is because of the grace of God. "But I repair cars. That's not a spiritual gift." I understand your thought, but your ability to fix a car actually comes from the way God made you (Exodus 35:30–35). If this is not true, then why is it that there are some of us who can barely figure out how to open the hood of a car, let alone read the oil dipstick?

Most of us take these abilities God designed us with for granted. We make comments like, "That's just the way I am." "That's easy, anybody can do that." Actually, the truth is that the talents many people take for granted are absolutely a gift from God, and others are amazed at that characteristic. It's interesting, but Father God gave me almost zero mechanical, artistic, and musical ability. I see people who know what direction to turn a light bulb and I stand in amazement. "Wow! How did they know how to do that?"

God specifically gave us every ability we have, or it would not come so easily to us. So whether we call them natural or spiritual, let's celebrate our gifts and thank Him for them.

His Talents

Your gifts and abilities are God-given. In the Parable of the Talents, Jesus indicated that they were originally the Host's talents (Matthew 25:14). He owned the talents and gave them to the contestants. Likewise, the talents you have been given were talents of Jesus. Wow! That's awesome! It almost seems as if He's insinuating that we were made in His image (Genesis 1:27)! What an honor to be given these talents that were originally His. Knowing they are directly from Him, we should certainly discover these gifts within us and then develop them.

Think about what you are naturally good at and how you can impact lives and bring glory to God through your unique characteristics. Also, think about how God has used you in the past. Many times this is because God is giving you favor or a special ability to relate to or connect with a specific demographic, like athletes, single parents, children, the elderly, and so on. Common sense will tell you that we won't be successful with people we can't relate to in life. Usually it is hard to deal with people with whom we have nothing in common.

Another thing that helps is to reflect on people for whom we have compassion. Many times this is the heart of God moving through us to help this group of people. Pay close attention to your energy level and heart; these can all be indications of how God is trying to guide you.

The more things that we can line up in our lives with our abilities and then match with the inner leading of the Holy Spirit, the better off we will be. As we move forward in these areas, let's continually be sensitive to the Spirit of God's guidance and direction. The compounded results over time can be astonishing.

The following are some discovery questions I believe will help you on this journey of finding the talents that God gave you and your purpose for them. If you already have an idea of what God has called you to do, it's still good to reflect on these questions. God can give you continued clarity on your life journey. These questions apply not only to vocation but also help point to areas of ministry (both inside and outside of the church) that God may be calling you to pursue. I would recommend you take some time to reflect on each question and write out or journal the answers. This can be very profitable in your process of moving forward.

Discovery Questions

1. What do you like to do?

    Think of activities that bring you fulfillment as you are doing them.

    Clean house, cook, make model airplanes, meditate, solve problems, train hamsters, fix cars, clean the attic, play music, decorate, or play sports? Organize, talk, listen, direct projects, study, or learn?

2. In what areas do you have natural strengths? What do you like to do?

    These are things are you naturally strong at and can say, "This is easy for me to do."

    Painting, reading, editing, graphic design, dancing, arranging flowers, social media, gardening, cooking, mechanics, communication, or computers?

3. What type of people do you feel comfortable around or have compassion for?

    What group of people does your heart say, "I wish I could do more for them"?

    The elderly, infants, motorcyclists, homeless, hurting, intellectuals, circus performers, NASA scientists, single moms, gang members, or cowboys?

4. How has God used you before to impact people?

   "Wow! God used me in that situation to speak wisdom to them and help solve that problem."

   Prayed for them, spoke truth to them, listened when they were going through trials, provided hospitality, ran errands for them, or helped them fix their car?

5. What things of God are you interested in?

   Perhaps you have experience in a particular area, or maybe you want to pursue training or involvement in a ministry.

   Music, teaching the Bible, missions, politics, children's ministry, hospitality, media, or helping behind the scenes?

6. What things has God spoken to you about in your life, or what things did someone else speak to you about that resonated inside of you?

   Maybe you always felt like you should be a pastor or a teacher. God spoke to you in a quiet time, when you were a child. Perhaps someone prophesied over you, or brought up a specific ability or demographic of people, and it seemed to hit a chord within you.

7. What things or activities consume you or give you passion and excitement?

   When you talk about them, you start feeling an increase in energy; maybe you speak faster, longer, or louder.

8. What opportunities do you have to connect with some of the above areas?

   Who do you know who is successful in these areas and how could you connect with them? How could you take a step forward?

   Calling, e-mailing, scheduling a meeting, or job shadowing?

Answers

Some people have had problems identifying their God-given abilities. Don't worry if this describes you. I believe that by answering the Discovery Questions, meditating on them, and listening to God's guidance, your abilities will become clear. God will not leave you hanging. His Word says, "Delight yourself also in the Lord, and He shall give you the desires of your heart" (Psalm 37:4, NKJV).

God wants you to identify your abilities, and He will help you so you can use them in your pursuit of hearing "Well done" from Him. Once we discover our talents, our job is to multiply them, like Contestants #1 and #2, to bring a maximum return for the kingdom of God. Let's talk about some of the steps we can take to get this kind of return.

MAC MAYER

Embracing Our Gifts

My life completely changed when I discovered the gifts with which God designed me, and I started embracing and developing them. Once I stopped allowing people to focus me on things I couldn't do, I had the freedom to think about what I could do. It took me a while, but soon I thought, *I'm different than other people and it's okay that I'm different.* People ask me why I hated school so vehemently from the day they dragged me to first grade until the joyous day at age sixteen, when I walked away. The whole thing was designed around things I wasn't wired to do well.

I finally came to the point, with self-reflection and God's help, of accepting myself for how I was made. I came to realize that I like to think about ideas and concepts. Instead of feeling bad or weird because I thought differently than my peers, I began to embrace that it was okay for me to be different. I may not know anything about car repair or opera, but in areas of dealing with people and business growth, it seems I naturally know the steps to take. Some of these traits I was born with, and some I learned over decades of honing these God-given abilities.

Recently, I spoke to a group of people on this subject and a forty-year-old guy came up to me afterwards and said, "Mac, that changed my life. I have been floundering all my life, struggling to improve the things I am bad at doing." Like many of us, he had heard that if he wanted to be successful, he had to develop the areas in which he wasn't so strong, instead of developing the areas in which he was naturally gifted. We put him through some basic assessments to find out his natural characteristics. He then had the peace and freedom to move forward, to begin taking real steps toward fulfilling his purpose in areas that he liked and was talented.

Let me clarify something. This does not excuse us from working on our weaknesses at all; it just means that we should focus the majority of our efforts on the things we are good at doing. I may not be very patient, but I still need to work at building up this trait, little by little, so I can show patience toward my wife, children, coworkers, and brothers and sisters in Christ. In the meantime, we should also be working on discovering and developing our strengths as well.

I recommend you first discover any potential good traits that you were given, and then start celebrating and embracing them. When I teach this, I say, "Find out your amazing qualities and wrap those traits around you like a warm blanket on a cold day. Just immerse yourself in the amazing beauty of how God made you. Celebrate it!" Really, I cannot tell you this enough. Let the wonderful characteristics that God made you with permeate every cell of your body and hold them close. If you are a people person, talk to and encourage as many people as you can! If you like music, rock on! If you are an artist, create! The Bible says, "As each one has received a gift, minister it to one another, as good stewards of the manifold grace of God" (1 Peter 4:10, NKJV). This means that God gave us all talents and abilities that we should use wisely to help others, so we can impact the world for Christ more effectively.

God loves it when we discover, embrace, and celebrate the amazing gifts that He so lovingly gave us to help others. He probably kicks back in His heavenly throne recliner with a huge smile on His face and beams, "Yep that's my son; that's my daughter; I'm so pleased they are using and enjoying the abilities I gave them."

If we are going to hear "Well done," we need to figure out what areas we are naturally gifted in and start developing them. God, the Master Designer, made us in a specific way, and He has a plan regarding how He wants us to use these talents. It is an insult to God when we diminish or put down how we are designed. We should recognize and rejoice in the abilities we have, which were given to us specifically by an amazing and loving God for a definite purpose.

Kingdom Use

In embracing our natural abilities and skills, there is a caveat. Just because we are good at something doesn't mean we should develop it. In school, I was good at drinking beer and chasing girls. This doesn't mean that my lifelong calling is to be an alcoholic playboy. That lifestyle would not prompt my Heavenly Father to declare "Well done!" Don't forget to ask yourself, *Will what I'm good at increase the success of the kingdom of God?*

I think we can all name some superstars within the sports and entertainment industries who have incredible, God-given talents. These highly gifted individuals are using their abilities, but they may or may not be using them to bring glory to God or edify others. However, everyone has a choice, and I'm not going to judge them for what they are doing with their gifts and abilities. That wouldn't do them or me any good. I am only responsible for me. I can pray God's enlightenment for them, but I need to focus on what God has called me to do.

WELL DONE

When I was young, I felt like my creative mind could solve almost any dilemma, even though I was not serving the kingdom of God. I thought, *I bet I can figure out how to remove all the Colonel Sanders memorabilia out of the local Kentucky Fried Chicken franchise, including the portrait of the Colonel, prominently located on the wall across from the cash register, and an authentic chicken barrel light fixture from the dining room ceiling during business hours without being discovered. My high school business teacher will be so impressed when I come to class with all the Kentucky Fried Chicken memorabilia. He is going to know how well I listened.* I was successful in removing all these things and more from the restaurant without anyone finding out—immediately, anyway. Ultimately, everyone was impressed, including the police and my parents; they just didn't celebrate my amazing accomplishment the way I had hoped.

Sometimes the outcome in our mind is far better than how it manifests in reality. That is probably one innovative thought that I should've just let pass on through my mind without action. The point is that we have the option of which kingdom we are going to use our gifts and abilities to promote and enhance. Just because we have a hammer doesn't mean everything is a nail. We can use the gifts of God in a positive way or a destructive way. The decision is ultimately ours. However, if we wish to hear "Well done" by the Host when He returns, we should stick to using these gifts in ways that honor God and bless others. If we are using our gifts and abilities for God, not only will we be laying up our treasures in heaven, but I believe we will experience success in our efforts on earth as well.

MAC MAYER

Pete Was Right!

When I was growing up, I learned one success principle that literally changed my entire life. This is a bold statement, but I believe there is one basic principle that is the key to all success in every area of life. I know, I'm sounding like those preachers with the "one key thing to success with God," but in all seriousness, this is one of the top things I like to talk about to help people move forward in life. Whether I'm talking to business leaders or church leaders, I like to ask how many of them have heard of the Peter Principle, and usually 20–40 percent say yes. Think about it! The key to success in virtually every area of life and only 20–40 percent of the people know about it.

First, the Peter Principle is not referring to Peter in the Bible. It is a concept coined by Laurence J. Peter, who stated in essence that we will progress in life to the level of our incompetency.[4] This means you can't succeed past your current competency level in any area of your life. This simple principle totally makes sense when you think about it. We haven't accomplished more in our lives because we don't have the understanding to get us there. The reason I'm not more successful in my marriage, my parenting, my finances, my health, my career, and my relationship with God is because my competency is lacking somewhere in these areas. Perhaps I need to become more knowledgeable in that area or maybe I need to work on self-control. Whatever it is, I will only advance in life to the level of my incompetence and not any further.

It's a very simple principle, but many people in the world don't want to admit that their success is based entirely on them. They want to rationalize that accomplishment is based on luck, their boss, or other things that are outside of their control. "Those rich, successful people are so lucky they were born into that family, went to that school, or married that person." "The only reason that guy is head of the music ministry is because he's the preacher's kid. I can sing and play a lot better than him." The list of excuses is endless. Part of taking ultimate accountability so we can grow is to accept responsibility for what is or isn't happening in our lives. This means I have to raise my skill level. Maturity says, "I'm the one and only one responsible for my results."

Excelling Past the Peter Principle

If you want to put the Peter Principle in your favor, I recommend you develop yourself past where you are in life. What if you made the commitment to out-work and out-develop yourself so far past where you are in life, that the Law of Compensation (also known as the Law of Sowing and Reaping—being compensated in proportion to that which you have contributed) kicked in and you couldn't be kept in your present position (Luke 6:38; Galatians 6:7)? What if you studied harder, worked harder, and mentally excelled far beyond your present position that it was impossible for you to stay at your current level?

Many people adapt to their present situation, saying, "Hey, I'm just working at this burger place. Why should I excel?" God's Word tells you to do your best, that's why. We've been instructed that "whatever you do, do it heartily, as to the Lord and not to men" (Colossians 3:23, NKJV). So, what if you actually did? What if you studied passionately in your chosen area? What if you worked your tail off? What if you fully developed in every area of your life and looked to be promoted? Do you really think you would stay at the drive-in window, handing out cholesterol packs in a bag? No, it's impossible. Doors and opportunities would open to you, no matter your race or gender.

Businesses and organizations are frantically looking for people to step up and bring them to a higher level, and if you can do it, they will hire you. If you make the most out of yourself and your situation by developing your gifts, your competency will skyrocket, and the success you will attain in life will be amazing. Remember, if people are more successful than us, it's not because they are lucky. Luck does not keep them in an elevated position; their competence allows them to maintain that position. Decide today that you will develop your skills and talents to their highest potential. It's a huge key in hearing, "Well done."

Increase Your Competency

So how do we go about raising our competency in the areas at which we are naturally gifted? We look for opportunities to increase our abilities. If you have a speaking or teaching gift, look for areas you can apply yourself. It's amazing how many large international ministries originally started as an in-home Bible study. This can be a great proving ground to develop your speaking skills and present your ideas. Get started, move ahead, and grow yourself. Is an organization or your church offering a class in an area where you need to progress? Then sign up! Maybe you will need to enroll in college or a Bible school. Whatever you need to do to increase your abilities, go after it. It will be worth it.

I know I seem to trash the concept of schools, but actually, I am a huge advocate for education. Two years ago, I felt like I really needed to develop my skills, so I spent almost $20,000 on education in one year. Before that, I spent a year taking night classes at a Bible college. Daily I'm reading books, listening to podcasts, and reading blogs. My goal is to listen to one growth-oriented audio book a week. Our growth is completely up to each one of us. We can raise proficiency and knowledge by taking classes, listening to audios and podcasts, reading, going to seminars, taking webinars, and a host of other things. Yet, competency is not just about what you know; it is about applying it.

Just because I have some ideas of what I should do with my life doesn't cut it. I actually have to increase my abilities to increase my results. Increasing our competency will not only increase our success on earth, but it is the key to hearing, "Well done" from the Reality Show Host at the end of our lives. Regardless of how many or how few talents we were given, the way we hear those joyous words is by actively investing in and increasing our abilities to bring a greater return for the kingdom of God.

Untapped Potential

Some of us may not recognize our talents and abilities because they are untapped. When I was a teen, I heard multiple people say, "You have so much potential." The sad part about this was I actually thought this was a compliment. People telling us we have potential is not a compliment; it's actually a slap in the face. What they're really saying in the politest way possible is, "I see some potential, but you aren't doing a darn thing with the abilities God gave you." They were ultimately saying, "You are wasting your life away, and I wouldn't want to be you when you have to account for all the unused potential that we see in you."

I also heard people say, "We don't pay for potential; we only reward based on results." Having potential and not doing anything with it is way worse than not having any potential at all and trying to do something with nothing. Think of Contestant #3. He had a talent, so we know he had potential, and what did he do with that talent? Zero, nada, zilch. He did the same thing I was doing—a big goose egg of nothingness. The only ability he had he buried, and I was doing the same thing. When I started developing my potential and skills, I was using them for the wrong kingdom. I would have gotten a reward, but it probably would've been swimming in my own lake of fire. It took me a while to accept God's love and understand that I should be using my abilities for a higher purpose. *Thank you, Jesus, for your mercy!*

Minimize Weaknesses

We know we're supposed to be developing our strengths and using them for God, but that doesn't mean we can forget about improving the areas in which we are weak. Our weaknesses (not necessarily academic) can actually counteract all of the positive impact that our strengths make in the world, if we do not figure out how to minimize or eliminate them. How many times have we heard about amazingly gifted people with a gigantic following, whose positive influence was undermined when their morality issue or character flaw was publicized? Their weakness damaged their ministry. In fact, their success elevated the visibility of their failure. We need to build our strengths and diminish or eliminate our weaknesses. If I'm weak in self-discipline or ethical areas, it can ruin my life completely. The sooner I work to eliminate these types of weaknesses, the better off I will be.

God said, "My grace is sufficient for you, for My strength is made perfect in weakness" (2 Corinthians 12:9, NKJV). If there is an area in life I struggle in, I need to fully acknowledge the problem right away, not bury my head in the sand. Next, I may need to get an accountability partner, pray, seek counseling, or engage in another form of treatment, but I need to start moving toward diminishing or eliminating the weakness before it destroys me. It is interesting, but often the people who can fully admit their failures and get victory over them gain a platform to help others through the same issues.

There may be other weaknesses in areas of your marriage, finances, health, children, reading, spelling, and so on. Once again, similar steps apply: fully admit there is a problem, pray, and take the necessary steps to minimize the weakness or problem so it does not prevent you from accomplishing God's plan for your life. You may be thinking, *I thought we were supposed to concentrate on building our strengths.* Yes, a majority of our time should be focused on developing our strengths; however, we must allow God to help eliminate strongholds that can hold us back from making a greater impact for His kingdom.

As previously noted, I am weak in several areas. I've had to take personal responsibility for my lack of competence in things like reading and writing. As much as I detested school, I did actually have to learn to read, write, and function in these areas at an acceptable level. By allowing God to help me minimize these weaknesses, while developing my strength of putting creative ideas together, now I'm able to share this book with you! We all have limitations, and some of them can cause devastating effects if we don't minimize them. Start now! Let's examine our lives to see what things could trip us up and take steps to diminish or eliminate these weaknesses in our lives.

MAC MAYER

Once we discover what we were designed to do, building up our strengths and minimizing our weaknesses, then we can start using our talents and abilities to a greater capacity. As we begin to use these abilities and are open to God's leading, He will guide and instruct us through His Spirit so we can move forward in fulfilling His plan for our lives.

WELL DONE

Reflection Questions

1. Did you learn anything new about yourself as you worked through the discovery questions earlier in the chapter? If so, what are some of your revelations?

2. In reflecting on the Peter Principle, what are three specific steps you can take to build your competence in your areas of gifting? What are you going to do this week?

3. Are there weaknesses in your life that could damage your life and undermine what God has called you to do? What are those weaknesses? What are some steps that you could take to begin eliminating them?

Chapter 6—Moving Forward Using Talents and Abilities

In the journey to fulfill God's plan for our lives, some people get stuck after discovering their talents and abilities because they can't decide whether it's God leading them or their own practical thoughts. They wind up confused, doubting what to do, and ultimately doing nothing—burying their talent like Contestant #3. This can be a realistic situation when we're seeking God's guidance; however, we can't let not knowing every step of God's direction for our lives keep us immobile and paralyzed with fear. It is true that we need to have God's peace and guidance as we pursue what He wants us to do, but it's also important for us to be practical and keep moving forward.

Spiritual Scavenger Hunt

If you take the time to prayerfully meditate on the Discovery Questions in Chapter 5, you will receive clues to your true-life scavenger hunt of discovering and fulfilling God's plan for your life. Be sensitive to what is going on inside of you, consciously aware of your emotions and reflections as you read the questions and think about or write out your answers. This is how God gives clues or directions. You may feel a gentle nudge inside of you. *Why don't you call that person, read that book, take that class, or go to that seminar?* That inner nudge is the clue for your next step in the scavenger hunt of personal growth.

Doing something is better than doing nothing to solve your life puzzle. Sometimes I will take a practical step just to discover, *Nope, I don't quite feel right about that direction; that is not where I will find my next clue. Okay, I need to try another direction.* We get the clues from prayer and sensing the Spirit of God's (also known as the Holy Spirit) direction, and the more we pray and are open to His direction, the easier it gets to sense our next move.

The Holy Spirit is a real person. He has a real personality and desires a strong relationship with us. When Jesus left the earth, the Holy Spirit was sent to us as a guide with wisdom and direction for our lives (John 14:26). Jesus said, "It is to your advantage that I go away; for if I do not go away, the Helper [Holy Spirit] will not come to you." (John 16:7, NKJV). Wow! It is pretty powerful that we are better off with the Holy Spirit than if Jesus were physically walking around with us. As part of God's promise to "never leave [us] nor forsake [us]" (Hebrews 13:5, NKJV), He sent the Holy Spirit who is always with us and will "guide [us] into all truth" (John 16:13, NKJV). As we communicate with each other differently, likewise, the Holy Spirit has a distinctly different relationship with each of us. The more we connect with Him, the more we sense His presence.

Endless Ways

While I describe how the Holy Spirit communicates with me and others I have talked to, understand that He may communicate with you in a unique way. There are no two identical flowers or snowflakes or ants. No two of anything in the entire universe is exactly the same; thus, no two individuals' relationships with the Holy Spirit are exactly the same.

God can speak directly to us, telling us to go a specific place where we will meet a specific person (Acts 8:29). He can also speak to us through music (Colossians 3:16), the Bible (2 Timothy 3:16), inanimate objects like clothing or art (1 Samuel 15:27–28; Jeremiah 18:1–10), other people via the gift of prophesy (Numbers 11:26–29), dreams (Acts 2:17), or a still small voice (1 Kings 19:12–13). For me, I must remain open to receive the guidance that He is always willing to give me. The more I mentally tune my mind toward God, the more I hear and sense His guidance.

As I turn the radio tuner in my head to the God channel by praying and reading His Word, His guidance becomes clearer (Psalm 119:105). However, there are many things that can block our spiritual radio connection with God, including doubt, fear, unforgiveness, sin, hate, and other destructive thoughts and distractions that prevent us from syncing our minds to His. It is embarrassing that we can get caught up in life, going days without thinking about the God of the universe who passionately wants a relationship with us. Yet as soon as we turn our thoughts and hearts toward Him, *bam!* There He is. He has been with us all the time.

The Bible says we are to be "bringing every thought into captivity to the obedience of Christ" (2 Corinthians 10:5, NKJV), so it is up to us to keep our mental tuner focused on thoughts toward God. He is always thinking loving thoughts toward us. We need to always be tuned in to receive what He has to say to us and how He wants to guide us.

Spiritual GPS

While the goal is to keep our thoughts tuned to the God channel, we don't need to be paranoid about making a wrong move and getting off track. God loves us and wants us back. In fact, He has given us our personal God's Positioning System (GPS), the Holy Spirit. If we are sensitive to Him and make a wrong turn, there is an inner voice or sense inside of us saying, *Okay, I should have turned there. I need to make a U-turn or get off at the next exit.* Don't worry if you have made wrong turns your entire life; God still wants to help you get back on track (Romans 8:28).

For years I ministered at our county jail, and I met people with a variety of charges from vagrancy to murder to child molestation. Many of these people felt they had gone past the limits of God's love, forgiveness, and grace. They believed their lives were over because they would be spending most or all of their remaining time on earth behind bars. I would tell them that if their god was not big enough to help them, then they needed a bigger God. We need God when we are in the worst part of our lives. Yes, we need Him in the good times too, but if things get too tough in our lives and our puny, fake god gets overwhelmed and bails on us, what kind of god is that? My God who created the universe says to just look to Him and He will guide us through the worst that life can throw at us (Deuteronomy 31:6, Hebrews 13:5).

Wherever you are, tune into the Holy Spirit GPS to sense God's guidance and look for the next turn to make. You don't have to memorize the next 1,500 miles of turns; the Holy Spirit has them memorized for you. Just take one direction at a time, and you will be back on track—moving toward fulfilling God's plan for your life.

Build the Car as You Drive It

When building a company or trying to help people move forward in their lives, I like to say, "We are building the car as we drive it." Think of how cars have developed over the years. What if Henry Ford would have proclaimed, "I'm not going to put cars on the market until we produce ones with power windows." You say, "Mac, that is absurd! They didn't know about power windows back then." Exactly! Life is about progression—starting small and growing into more complex ideas. Yet, many people want to start off with all of the answers before they even begin their journey saying, "I'm not moving forward until I know every detail of this trip and have it mapped out." Ford had to start out by manufacturing the four-cylinder, fifteen-horsepower Model N. The success of this vehicle led him to produce a more complex four-cylinder, twenty-horsepower Model T. Later, he moved on to make bigger, faster, and more luxurious cars.[5] This progression to more complex ideas continues today as we now have self-driving cars.

On our journey toward hearing, "Well done," we don't need to know how everything up ahead will work out. I see too many people procrastinating and spending years intricately plotting out a plan that, by the time they get around to implementing, is obsolete. We just need to move forward, and when we see a way to progress, then we can take that next step.

Mistakes Have Value

Sometimes when we take the next step, we make mistakes, but that's okay. I tell organizations or people I coach that mistakes can be good. Understand, this is not something I say just because it might sound interesting or provocative. I really believe it. I'm totally ecstatic when someone is willing to risk doing something out of the ordinary that could result in a mistake. Society mocks people who make mistakes. I'm *looking* for people who have the inner drive to actually try something different that may not succeed. This speaks volumes. Taking these risks helps us find out what doesn't work. It's very important to see what braking system doesn't work on our car, so it will help us to discover what will work.

Thomas Edison, inventor of the electric light bulb, phonograph, and motion picture camera, was certainly not afraid to make mistakes. He once said, "If I find 10,000 ways something won't work, I haven't failed. I am not discouraged, because every wrong attempt discarded is often a step forward."[6] We have to try unsuccessful option #1, before we can get enough knowledge to come up with a solution that will work.

Mistakes are opportunities for growth. If I know what people are having problems with, I can help them advance in life through coaching; however, if they hide their mistakes from me or won't acknowledge them, I can't help. Transparency is the key. If we're allowed to make mistakes that are openly discussed without judgment, by others and ourselves, then we can come up with solutions. Generally, the more successful a person is, the more mistakes they have made. Successful people learn from what they did wrong and keep moving. It comes back to Newton's First Law of Motion—objects in motion tend to stay in motion unless acted upon by an outside force. This is the secret to their success, keeping the momentum going by moving forward.

You may say, "What about prayer? Won't we get things right if we pray?" Obviously I believe in prayer and find it extremely important to wait on God's answer before making a major life decision. However, so many people are "waiting on the Lord" to tell them which business they should send their résumé, whether or not they should invite their neighbor to church, or even when to step off the sidewalk to cross the street. If I stopped to ask God if I was making the right decision before every action throughout the day and waited on each answer, I might only accomplish a few tasks all day long. I don't think this is what God has in mind for us. The idea is to be in tune to the Holy Spirit's leading, but if we don't hear Him constantly speaking, keep progressing, keep moving. What harm will it do to hand out your résumé to several companies? Doesn't the Great Commission tell us to "Go therefore and make disciples of all the nations" (Matthew 28:19, NKJV)? There's your answer to whether or not to invite your neighbor to church this Sunday.

As long as our actions are in line with God's Word and we remain tuned in to the Holy Spirit, it's okay to make some decisions on our own. We can take comfort that if we haven't heard an answer from God, His Word says that if we seek Him with all our heart, we will find Him (Jeremiah 29:13). He will speak to us. Until then, we should continue to move forward, using His Word as our guide, so we won't be accused of being lazy like Contestant #3. When we do make mistakes, we won't be thrown completely off track. Rather, these minor mistakes will help us learn and lead us to eventually hearing, "Well done."

Start Small

I appreciate your heart to change the world as you move forward; however, before you decide to rent coliseums across the continent for your evangelistic crusades, it's okay to start small with your idea to see if it works. We always want to seek God's guidance, but the Bible asks, "For who has despised the day of small things?" (Zechariah 4:10, NKJV). Jesus also reminded us, "He who is faithful in what is least is faithful also in much" (Luke 16:10, NKJV). Unless God specifically tells us to start off on a larger scale, we might want to start an in-home Bible study or some other small step to learn what works and what does not work, gradually moving ahead.

I know we all want to transform the world next week, but there is real wisdom in figuring out if our ideas work and advancing them as God gives us additional guidance and favor. We will make less costly mistakes, lower our risk, and ultimately have more success because we will not be continually starting over or wasting resources. Even if God has given me a great vision to accomplish something, wisdom would ask, "Okay, what's the next step I could take to progress toward achievement?"

Convergence

Another favorite subject I like to talk about is convergence. The concept of convergence is life changing. Once you understand the idea, you will see that it is the reason for gigantic success throughout history, and it can also be a key to success in your vocational endeavors, spiritual goals, and your ultimate achievement of hearing "Well done" from the One who gave you your amazing abilities.

Convergence is where multiple lines cross, meet, or intersect. As an example, the first line represents us discovering and developing our special traits and abilities. When we intersect these God-given traits with the second line, which are the tangible needs of other people (often providing an answer to their prayers), this can result with their lives being changed by a talent of which we were made a steward. This is a vital key to business success, church success, kingdom success, and your personal success. So line

#1 is our God-given traits and abilities intersecting with line #2, representing a need or an answer to someone's situation.

In sports, people use the term "sweet spot" when the ball is hit in the center of the tennis racket, baseball bat, or golf club, allowing it to go farther with less effort and more accuracy. In other sports, athletes call it the "zone," meaning all their energies are focused in an almost supernatural way for maximum results. It's like they couldn't fail. While this can produce impressive outcomes in sports, when used for the kingdom, convergence can have eternal results.

Connecting our talents with others' needs is powerful; however, the real strength comes in with line #3, which is the God factor. This comes when we ask, "What does God want to do or what is He doing in which we can take part?" Let's put the concepts together through a sequence of questions.

WELL DONE

The Trinity Convergence

In order to discover and apply the elements of convergence in our own lives, we should be asking "what" questions. Because I'm a businessman, I write from a business perspective. The basic concept for business success is to find a need and fill it. Therefore, the first line of questions we should ask are about the needs around us.

Convergence Questions for Line #1: Need

- What does our community need?

- What do people around me need?

- What would make their lives better?

This should be followed up by a second set of more introspective questions about our abilities.

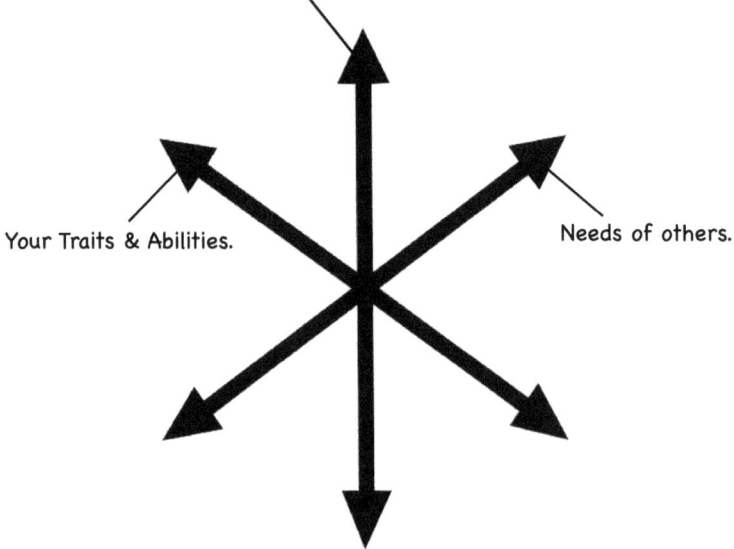

What does God want to do?

Your Traits & Abilities.

Needs of others.

MAC MAYER

Holy Spirit

- What is the Holy Spirit doing?
- What does the Holy Spirit want to do?
- What need does God want to meet?
- What ministries or organizations is the Holy Spirit working through?
- What segment or market do I know where the Holy Spirit is either currently doing something significant or wants to impact?

But how do you know what the Holy Spirit wants to do? The answer is found through prayer. I say, *Holy Spirit, show me what you want to do.* I also observe where God is currently moving. Where are lives visibly being changed through the power of God? Once we get through asking the what questions, we can then begin to pray that God will reveal how He will solve the need. *Father, I know You have given me talents and abilities that I can use to help people in need. Help me discover **what** abilities I have, show me **what** answers I can help with, and reveal to me **how** You want me to use my abilities to solve a need and bring glory to You.*

When we are directed by the Holy Spirit to use our talents to impact someone's life, it's like we're in the zone, a supernatural convergence, accomplishing God's will in the sweet spot of our abilities. This puts us on the right track to fulfill His will for our lives.

Think of the power this creates! If someone is crying out to God saying, "Father, we need an answer. Please help us." The Father wants to help us and answer our prayer (John 15:7; Matthew 7:7–8). The Father then looks around to see who Jesus has given His abilities to so He can send and flow His Spirit through to answer their prayer. Who is willing and available to be His pipeline to them, helping Him answer their request with a yes and amen (2 Corinthians 1:20)? God is looking for people who are ready, willing, and gifted by Him to be His conduit to the world through which He can answer their prayers. Think about it. We get the honor of being God's answer to their prayer!

The better we utilize our abilities to impact people's lives by God's direction, the more tangible the energy God releases into a life-changing situation.

Convergence Examples

Here is an outrageous example of our abilities converging with people's needs, just to show you how it works. Let's say I'm the best circus juggler in the world. I can juggle more objects, a wider variety of them, and faster than anyone else on the planet. I can juggle them while driving, swimming, and getting my teeth cleaned. I can juggle toothpicks and even running chain saws; I'm absolutely amazing at juggling. But how do I use such an unusual gift to advance the kingdom of God? Obviously this is a God-given gift, since no one has ever been able to juggle like I can. With such an extraordinary gift, the big question is, do I use it for worldly or spiritual success?

Since my talent is entertaining, one of my options is to use it as a Las Vegas performer, selling out shows for years to come and gaining great riches and personal acclaim. That is not necessarily bad, since it gives me the option to use the millions of dollars I make any way I want, including for the kingdom of God. Of course, I could also use it for a corrupt lifestyle of parties if I choose to do so. I decide to prayerfully brainstorm additional ways I can converge my ability with people's needs in a life-changing way for the kingdom of God. I don't mind making mistakes because I know the process can lead me to more ideas.

The Discovery Questions in chapter 5 remind me that I know other amazingly God-gifted entertainers who also want to use their abilities for the kingdom of God, and because we all believe in walking in unity like the Bible indicates, we decide to work together. We run into other people who have administrative gifts, marketing gifts, and ministry gifts, and we all decide to prototype our idea and start small by creating an entertaining outreach event in our community with the main purpose of telling people about Christ. We try it on a limited basis and make smaller mistakes from which we can learn and grow. This process empowers us to make additional changes, and gradually we all move forward to great success by impacting millions of people for the kingdom of God. Eventually, all of us hear, "Well done."

As you can see with this example, there are thousands of variations to how we could use our abilities, which is why we need the GPS wisdom of the Holy Spirit. The Holy Spirit may want us to stay in Las Vegas to be a light of truth in a dark place or choose a thousand different options along the way. For our success, there is a balance of practical and spiritual. God doesn't tell me every detail; that is why I need to take practical steps in my pursuit of fulfilling His plan for my life. However, the wisdom and Spirit of God are my default because He knows details I can't see in my practical mind. The sign ahead says "The bridge is out," but my spiritual GPS says keep going. All I can say is let's keep going; it's going to be a memorable ride.

You might ask, "What if I'm not the greatest juggler in the world? What if I'm not the greatest anything? What then?" Everyone is important in the body of Christ (1 Corinthians 12:12–31). Even in our example, it may take hundreds of people working together to make the events successful. Consider David and his mighty men. Everyone shared in the rewards even if they were left to guard the camp (1 Samuel 30:24–25). Think of a normal church service where one guy is up on stage delivering a message of God. Yet there are hundreds of people behind the scenes—equally as important—working together to put on such a great church service. If someone hadn't unlocked the doors, turned on the lights, and adjusted the thermostat, it might not have taken place. Many people gave of their tithes and offerings to keep lights on and pay for the facility. People in the children's and music ministries did their part as well. All parts are important in making the service successful. There are no insignificant gifts in the kingdom of God; you and your talents are greatly needed.

The Journey Continues

In this chapter, we learned how to use the gifts we have previously identified and move those forward by listening to the Holy Spirit, understanding that it is okay if we make mistakes. Our Holy Spirit GPS will continue to help us get back on the right path, moving forward in our quest to hear, "Well done." As we do this, convergence is set into motion, allowing God's power to move through the characteristics He's given us and being an integral part of the answer to someone's prayers. Wow! What an amazing honor to be used by God with our talents and be a part of God's solution for their request. If we want to experience these powerful situations of convergence, we should not only follow God's leading, but we must take responsibility for our actions and the abilities He's given us.

Reflection Questions

1. How have you experienced the Holy Spirit guiding you?

2. What are some mistakes you have made that have been huge opportunities for learning and growth?

3. Answer the questions from the Trinity Convergence. What are three small steps you can take to start putting the concept of convergence into action for the kingdom?

Chapter 7—I Am Responsible for Me

Successful leadership begins with taking responsibility for our thoughts and actions. If we can't lead ourselves, it will limit our success at leading others and our overall success as well. Remember what the flight attendant says in the preflight instruction? "Place the oxygen mask over your nose and mouth before you assist others." Once this basic need is met, then we can help someone else. The Reality Show Host said it this way: "First remove the plank from your own eye, and then you will see clearly to remove the speck from your brother's eye" (Matthew 7:5, NKJV). If we work on ourselves first, people will be more likely to listen and respect us as a leader. This concept applies to all elements of our lives, from our physical bodies to our finances, to our thoughts, attitudes, actions, and relationships.

This sounds so simple, but unfortunately it seems like society is geared toward making us victims. Society goes out of its way to avoid hurting our feelings by saying, "Your behavior isn't your fault. If your mommy had burped you differently when you were a baby, your whole life would be different today. You poor thing! Let society take care of you now, while we give you lots of free things all embroidered with your own personalized victimization logo." The truth is there comes a time in our lives when we need to take the pacifier out of our mouths, grow up, and take responsibility for how we think, speak, and act.

Accountability

The Jewish age of accountability is thirteen years old for a boy, which is celebrated by a "coming of age" party called a bar mitzvah. Jewish girls celebrate at age twelve with a bat mitzvah. In our society, there seems to be no age of accountability. If we choose, we can be like Peter Pan and never grow up or be held responsible for our lives. As a result, there are hundreds of thousands of adolescents walking around in adult bodies, clueless about growing up. The effect on our society is enormous.

Anytime we don't accept the consequences of our actions and place them anywhere except on ourselves, we lose the power to change or be different. If we say the reason why we're acting this way is because of what *they* did to us, then we are purposely giving *they* the power over us. Essentially, we are saying that their influence on us has more power than our own influence has over our lives.

What if we did something really crazy and accepted complete responsibility for *all* areas of our lives? What if we took that crazy idea one step further, accepting full responsibility for absolutely everything in our *world*? What if anytime we looked at any part of our lives, we first looked at ourselves as the problem instead of thinking we had no control in that area?

For instance, if I become seventy-five pounds overweight, I can't blame the fast-food industry—it's **my** fault. I drove in, paid the money, and wolfed down a double order of cheese-drenched fries and washed it down with a family-size barrel of cola every day for the last year. The reason I have a high balance on my credit card is **me**. I charged the large tub

WELL DONE

of fries floating in cheese and the soda barrel on my credit card, making excuses like, I couldn't live without them and I didn't have any cash in my wallet.

Ultimately, no matter what happened, it's my fault and my behaviors are the only ones to blame. The refreshing thing about this viewpoint is that if I'm the one to blame, I'm also the one who can solve the problem. It saves a lot of time. I don't need to look any further than myself to make changes in my life.

What if the next time someone started complaining about the government, we had the mentality, "Yep, I know. That's my responsibility." What if we responded by saying, "Look, I believe in ultimate personal responsibility. I can't assign blame to them when I haven't done everything I can to fix the problem myself." Since we can't go back and rewrite history, it's a waste of time to get caught up in the could-have or should-have mind-set. Instead, I can look in the mirror and ask myself, *Next time around, what can I do to make a difference? Can I vote? Can I pray about the situation? Can I actively participate in the election? Can I encourage others to vote? Can I raise money and support the people I believe are the best candidates?*

Wouldn't it be refreshing if, instead of being a victim and complaining about everything, we took responsibility for our actions? We may not be able to influence everything in the world, but unless we take responsibility for what we can do, we aren't actually taking responsibility at all. Would this make a difference in your marriage? It's not about what my spouse could do differently; it's only about how I can behave differently. It's not about what your pastor, your boss, or your best friend should change; it's only about how you can make positive adjustments to your thoughts and actions in order to bring about better results.

Influencers

As we continue to make these adjustments and change our mind-set, it's helpful to look at the things around us that either try or succeed at influencing us. We watch TV commercials and soon we run out of the house that we found through a realtor advertised on a billboard. We get into our car that we bought when we saw it on one of those ridiculously expensive ads during the Super Bowl, and go to get teeth whitener that was one of the household products on our favorite game show. Then we chow down a triple-stacked hamburger from a burger joint with the memorable jingle we heard on the radio, and finish out our errands by getting our prescription filled for a drug we saw on an Internet site we frequent daily, a drug with side effects that are worse than the ailment. We do all of this, only to come home and dial a phone number we saw during a late-night marathon of our favorite reality show to join a class action lawsuit on the same prescription we just got filled that is supposed to offset the effects of eating too many hamburgers.

None of these media outlets may be intrinsically wrong, but we just gave our control to someone else and they are influencing our power of choice. I allowed others to influence me when they cut me off in traffic and I gave them the one-finger salute, and then I blamed them for making me give them that salute. The truth is they didn't make me do anything. It's *my* finger, stuck to *my* hand, controlled by *my* brain, and the words that I muttered under *my* breath came out of *my* mouth, which was oddly enough connected to the same brain that directed my finger, even though it didn't appear that my brain was connected during either one of those events.

The things we allow ourselves to see and hear influence us. They seep into our subconscious and we begin to meditate on them until they manifest into actions. This is why the Bible tells us, "Whatever things are true, whatever things are noble, whatever things are just, whatever things are pure, whatever things are lovely, whatever things are of good report, if there is any virtue and if there is anything praiseworthy—meditate on these things" (Philippians 4:8, NKJV). Leading ourselves the way God expects means being responsible for what we allow into our minds, because eventually what goes in will come out.

It's All My Responsibility

As part of my coaching business, I was hired by a rapidly growing organization to be, in effect, the acting CEO. In one of the early staff meetings, I announced, "I want you to know that everything that happens here is my responsibility." I said, "If the toilets overflow, it's my responsibility. If there is garbage on the floor of the bathroom, that would be my responsibility. Everything that goes wrong is my responsibility." The staff looked at me like I had been visiting the states where marijuana had been legalized.

You ask, "Mac, why would you say that?" It's because it is true. Your practicality responds by saying, "You can't help it if someone throws garbage on the bathroom floor or the toilet overflows." Actually, that's an excuse. If I'm a leader, ultimately I'm responsible for everything. If I don't want paper towels on the bathroom floor, I can remove them and put in hand dryers. If there is still a problem in the bathroom, maybe I should assign a monitor to be there. If the toilets overflow, maybe they need to be replaced. No matter what the problem, if I take responsibility for it, then I have the power to solve it. Otherwise, I become powerless to bring about change, and I become a victim.

Lucky the Dog

The other day, I saw a poster that read, *Lost Dog: 3 legs, blind in one eye, missing right ear, tail broken, recently neutered. Answers to the name of "Lucky."*

Right away, I saw the parallel between this poster and some people's lives, including a biblical character. When I think of Lucky the Dog, it reminds me of Paul. *Apostle of God: beaten with rods and whips, stoned and left for dead, shipwrecked, adrift at sea for a day and night, cold, hungry, imprisoned without cause. Answers to the name of "Paul."*

He was responsible for writing much of the New Testament and influenced billions of people for Christ. Before he was likely beheaded by Nero, he was last seen chained at the bottom of a cold, damp cave they called a jail and singing praise songs about his blessings. Remind me again what our excuse was for not doing something impactful for the kingdom of God with our posh life?

Paul talked of his adversities as character-building opportunities. He said, "We also glory in tribulations, knowing that tribulation produces perseverance; and perseverance, character; and character, hope" (Romans 5:3-4, NKJV). If Paul's life can make Lucky the Dog's life look really good and blessed, why are we looking at our trivial inconveniences as a big deal? We choose what thoughts we allow ourselves to think. Perhaps we should focus on the good things in our lives, like God loves us and He has an awesome plan for our lives.

WELL DONE

Devastation or Adventure

As you can tell from the Apostle Paul's story, perception is everything. While I am in no way comparing my life story to his, I find that it may help some readers understand that you can choose how to view your life story, and this perception will determine your outcome.

Dianne and I went through a huge financial collapse, lost millions of dollars, and literally everything we owned, including cars and our home. Can you say bummer? The following is a condensed account of what happened to us during that time in the form of a pretend letter from my wife.

Mac,

I'm glad you accomplished the previous honey-dos of starting multiple companies, owning dozens of properties, becoming a multimillionaire and being financially free in your forties.

Now, could you stop by the ER while you're in shock from a freak accident and a dislocated shoulder? Tell them I will pop in later for emergency surgery, having had a burst appendix for three days. Don't worry—I will survive by the grace of God, but there will be thousands in medical bills that we won't be able to pay. Let the bank know where the keys are to our fancy cars, homes, office buildings, and second home in Sun Valley. Please apologize to them because we didn't get time to clean them before handing them over.

Before I forget to tell you, I just heard from our son. He got three more years in prison. Also, your eighty-year-old mom called—your dad died. She also mentioned that she is plan-

ning a Life Flight trip to the ER with brain trauma, and she was wondering why the courts want to take away the home that you paid off for them.

I just got a call from the real estate commission, appraisal board, IRS, and a multitude of attorneys. They want tens of thousands of pages of documentation about our lives over the last twenty years. When you get a moment, can you put that together? Put on the calendar that you will be fruitlessly interrogated for countless hours, month after month. People will mock and ridicule you, and you'll find your name in the newspapers and the subject of radio talk shows, scorning all of the work that we've done for thousands of people transitioning out of jails and prisons.

One last thing: since you were gone, your partners called. They are taking the company that you personally started over thirty years ago, along with all of our income.

Love, Dianne

P.S. Since all of our savings, investments, income, cars, and properties are gone, could you catch a ride to the church and get a food box for Thanksgiving and Christmas? Thanks!

    The world would tell Dianne and me how terrible it was that we were multimillionaires with businesses, real estate, and a second home at a resort and now we have nothing. Remember, it was up to us to decide how we would perceive these events and what label we would put on them. To say that we were hurt and confused would be a major understatement. It hurt terribly to see our life's work taken away through multiple events. It was like the perfect storm, or rather the Bermuda Triangle, where everything was gone in a very public way. Naturally, these events had us asking a ton of fruitless "why" questions (I will expand on this concept later in the chapter).

Many couples who go through things like this end up divorced, turn away from God, and become bitter. Dianne and I decided we would recommit our lives to each other and to God. We determined to have a stronger marriage and a closer relationship with God.

Gradually, we came to the conclusion that it was up to us to decide how we were going to perceive what had happened in our lives. How would we label these events and our new life ahead? The first word that came to my mind was "devastation." Our lives were devastated. Every area of our lives had been ransacked and torn to smithereens. We literally had nothing left, and our self-images were in the toilet. Devastation seemed to describe our situation, but it didn't exactly have a positive ring to it. We finally picked the word "adventure" and put that label on what we were going though. Dianne and I get to have a Great Adventure together!

We would say, "Wow! This is going to be so cool to see how God provides for us. It's going to be exciting to see how God gets us food, a place to live, and money." People would say, "Mac, aren't you worried?" I would reply, "What do I have to worry about? It's God's problem, not mine. His Word says, "[He] shall supply all [our] need" (Philippians 4:19, NKJV) and also "seek first the kingdom of God and His righteousness, and all these things shall be added to [us]" (Matthew 6:33, NKJV). It's His promise, and He will take care of us no matter what situation we are in. I just refused to worry. Every time negative thoughts came into our minds, we had to consciously replace them with, *This is God's problem, not ours. We are on a great adventure to see God's goodness. We never would've got a firsthand understanding of all of these experiences of life, like being homeless for six weeks and praying for each meal, if this never had happened to us.*

I told this personal story not to gain sympathy but to show you the power of perception. If we had allowed the world to influence us to view ourselves as complete failures and become devastated because of these events, we would've missed out on experiencing the tangible blessings we received, the many friendships we have made, as well as a greater capacity to minister to others. Thank God for His loving kindness!

Dad, the Phone Is for You

I may be dating myself a bit, but back in the day, when a guy named Alexander Graham Bell lived, people had phones that hooked to the wall by a cord; I presume it was a security thing so no one would misplace or steal them. As very young children, we began to notice the phone. The phone would ring, and people would answer it. Yet how many times, as a three-year-old, was the phone for you? Maybe Grandma and Grandpa would call to wish you a happy birthday, but you're right—very rarely did you get a call at that age.

Yet when you were older, every once in a while when you heard the ring, you would get brave and say, "I'll get it!" Mimicking the adults you'd seen do this hundreds of times before, you said, "Hello, uh, this is Timmy." The person on the other end responded with, "This is collections and I'm calling to see when the payment will be made." With full confidence that you knew exactly who could help this person on the other end of the phone, you replied, "Okay, let me get my dad." Your dad came over, took the phone and said to the caller, "Okay sure, I'll get that handled right away."

Cool story Mac, so what's the point? We are taking mental phone calls every day that are really not ours to handle. Instead, we should be handing the phone to our Dad and saying, "Look, this is for you." I get ringing thoughts in my head like, *How are you going to pay that repair bill?* I just look toward my Father God and say, "Dad, you said you would take care of me. This thought is for you." Some mental phone calls are persistent because they are used to talking to me. Now every time they call, I give them to Father God. I just refuse to talk to them or even worry about them. That doesn't mean I don't do what I can to resolve the situation on my end. It means I've just decided I'm not going to worry about the thoughts surrounding the situation. I'm going to hand the thoughts to my Father. Dad handles a lot of mental phone calls, but what is weird is the more I hand the phone off to Him, pretty soon they are calling less and I have way more peace.

Give Thanks

One way to keep a handle on our thought life is to "give thanks in all circumstances" (1 Thessalonians 5:18, ESV). I'm not saying we should rejoice when someone gets hurt or bad things happen. In those situations, we should rejoice that God loves them, knows their situation, has not forgotten them, and will create all things for good if they allow Him. In Jesus, there is always something to be thankful for, and we should focus on and give praise for those things. I can consciously make the decision to praise God on what appears to be my darkest days, because the reality is I am still steadfastly loved by God and get to spend eternity in His presence. There is always a reason to praise God, and that gives us cause to meditate on His good and pleasing will for our lives.

Why

Fortunately, Dianne and I understood the power of praise and got through the "questioning God" phase fairly quickly. Yet, many waste so much time asking that age-old question, *why* with the wrong mind-set. *Why* is one of the most powerful questions a person can ask. The question *why* has changed man's perception of the earth and instigated millions of inventions. Unfortunately, when asked in a certain context, *why* is also one of the most detrimental questions a person can ask. The mind is very powerful and if we ask it a question, it will manufacture an answer. The question you ask determines what answer you get.

Here's how it works. I have a fight with my wife and the following negative question goes through my mind: **Why don't you get along with your wife?** My mind is programmed to come up with answers to questions, even though the question is asked in a terrible way. My mind starts racing for a multitude of answers as to why we don't get along. *She is a nag; she doesn't really understand you; you married the wrong woman; you weren't meant to be together*, and on and on.

A more positive question would be, **What** *could I do differently so Dianne and I will get along?* Okay, I could spend more time with her, be more patient, love her unconditionally. I could also ask the question, **How** *could I get along* *better with Dianne?* These questions put me in a problem-solving mode.

Many people don't realize that asking a *why* question about past events puts us in a victim mentality. If we ask why in a negative context, we will get a negative answer. *Why don't I get along with my boss? Why didn't I get the raise? Why did that event happen to me?* The question you ask determines the answer you will get, and if you ask a bad question, you will get a bad answer. Our goal should be to ask positive questions that focus on solutions. This is a simple yet powerful approach that will help us respond properly to events in our lives to bring about more positive outcomes.

"You" Algebra

According to author and motivational speaker John Maxwell, "Everything rises and falls on leadership."[7] So, if we're responsible for our own lives and things aren't working, we need to look in the mirror and make the changes necessary to obtain different results.

Leading yourself is the ultimate algebra problem, and the only factor in the equation that you can change is, drum roll—**You**. By ultimately changing the you factor of your life equation, you change the entire outcome of your life's results. When we have this viewpoint, our whole perception of the problems we face changes, and we're free to be part of the solution instead of at the mercy of conditions beyond our control. We just have to think about how we can change ourselves to affect a different outcome.

When we take responsibility of our lives and view situations not as the world sees them, but as God promises, we are no longer living in fear like Contestant #3 (Matthew

25:25), but in faith like Contestants #1 and #2. They took responsibility and multiplied the talents that the Host gave them, believing that He would return and expect to see increase in the talents. Their reward for their faithful actions was to be made rulers over many things (Matthew 25:21, 23). Likewise, when we are faithful with what Father God has given us, He can then promote us to leadership positions.

Before He can promote us, we have to take full responsibility for our thoughts and actions and tune in to the Holy Spirit's guidance so we can move forward. This will always be our top priority. We are always leading in some capacity, whether or not we recognize and admit it. Our coworkers, our children and other young people, our friends and peers are all looking at how we behave and learning from our actions. We are all leaders, unless we're hermits hidden away in a distant mountain cave having no contact with humanity; some just lead in a more direct and larger capacity. So let's take the next step in seeing how our life can make a positive impact on others.

Reflection Questions

1. What are some outside influencers that you have been listening to? How has this impacted your decision-making in your career, home, ministry?

WELL DONE

2. How have you seen God working in your life and on your behalf during situations or events that may have felt devastating?

3. Have you ever gotten stuck in questioning why? Where did that lead you? How did you get past it?

4. Are there some mental phone calls you need to hand over to your Father?

Chapter 8—Learning to Lead

The Bible is full of examples of average people God chose to become great leaders because they were "faithful over a few things" (Matthew 25:21, 23, NKJV). He chose David to be king of Israel over his seven older and physically capable brothers because David was a man after God's own heart (1 Samuel 13:14, 16:1–13). He chose Moses, the humblest man on earth, to lead the Israelites out of Egypt and into the Promised Land (Numbers 12:3). He chose Esther, a young Jewish woman who would eventually stand up to the king for her people and save them from extermination to be queen of Persia because He saw that she was respectful and obedient to the authority figure in her life, her cousin Mordecai (Esther 2:10).

Even if we are not the most charismatic, eloquent, or intellectual people, God can still mold us into effective leaders if we are building a solid relationship with Him, continue to avoid Satan's traps, and are faithful with the abilities we have been given. Over the years, I have heard many people, both in the church and in professional settings, ask the following questions: "Why don't they promote me?" "Why haven't they chosen me to be a leader? I've been here way longer than the people who are in charge now." "What's wrong with me?" Let's talk about a few things that hold people back from fulfilling God's call on their lives and discovering how they cannot only hear "Well done," but be selected as one of those rulers over many things.

Honesty

As an employer, business coach, and church administrator, the main quality I look for in people is honesty. At one time, I was a partner in a very large drug treatment facility with hundreds of clients. Most of our clients came from jails and prisons. Our hearts went out to these amazing men and women caught up in the bondage of drugs. We wanted to do everything we could to see people reach their God-given potential. Over time, I discovered that the major character issue that blocked their success was a lack of complete honesty. They said things they thought their counselor wanted to hear, they made up stories, and they wouldn't admit they were struggling in certain areas. It was just a matter of time before the truth came out, and unfortunately many went back to prison as a result.

I've seen multiple people whose pride kept them from admitting their marriage was in trouble, their finances were a wreck, or they had other issues that were keeping them from progressing in life. If they would've been vulnerable and honest about their situation and asked for help, it could have been resolved. If we can be honest with all-knowing Father God and with those who can help us on our life journey, then we can progress.

One habit I'm developing is immediately clearing up inaccurate information once I find out what I said wasn't completely correct. In these situations, I don't have to come out and say, "Hey, I lied to you." Instead, I use a softer version such as, "Hey, I misspoke in this situation. Here is the accurate information." It feels so good to step up and own the situation, setting the record straight with the truth. After I made myself do this a few times, it encouraged me to provide accurate information the first time around. God's Word says, "Those who deal truthfully are [God's] delight" (Proverbs 12:22b, NKJV). Make it a habit to be completely honest. It might be uncomfortable, but it's an essential trait and a key to your success as a godly leader.

Faithfulness

During one phase of our life, Dianne and I drove two hours one way to church almost every Sunday for two years. We felt that we were supposed to move to a new community, but we didn't feel that God had given us the peace to leave the church we were attending. So, each Sunday we drove back and forth. People would ask us, "Isn't that a great inconvenience for you to drive four hours round-trip to church?" Why should we look at this as an inconvenience at all? The road Jesus took to the cross at Calvary, now *that* was inconvenient! I'm so glad He did though. Each week, we got to drive back and forth in an air-conditioned car, hold each other's hand, and listen to praise music while drinking a cup of coffee. Sounds almost like heaven to me!

In our society, faithfulness is an uncommon characteristic. It means showing up on time, every time, keeping your word, offering true and constant support, and being dependable. Contestants #1 and #2 were called faithful servants in the Parable of the Talents and were made rulers over many things (Matthew 25:21,23). As an employer, whenever I look at a résumé to hire someone, one of the first attributes I look for is their faithfulness to their previous employers. Did they change jobs every few months or years, or seem to move from town to town? Faithfulness creates longevity and cohesiveness within groups or organizations. Faithful employees or group members generally stand out among their coworkers or fellow members and are often the first to receive a promotion.

Accountability

Closely related to faithfulness is the idea of accountability. It's probably my age, but our society seems to have generally declined in the area of accountability over time. The Bible says our character should be such that we don't go back on our word (Psalm 15:4). I totally agree with this unless I change my mind. *Oops!* I can think of times when I've completely blown this principle and have taken the wimpy way out. Years later, I still feel bad that I didn't fulfill my promises.

Accountability was literally beaten into me from my German heritage. My dad had very rigid beliefs about hard work and doing what you were supposed to do, no excuses. "Mac, you mowed the lawn and it's not totally even. Mow it again." I started my first full-time job at twelve years old, mowing the lawns at a large apartment complex. When all of the adults kept quitting, they hired me. I can remember at sixteen years old having to get out of bed at 1:30 in the morning and go across town to re-clean bathrooms at a gas station I worked at because they were not done properly. I was taught concepts such as "your word is your bond" and "you are only as good as your word." You can call me old-fashioned, but accountability is an admirable trait that will help you advance as a leader if you are 100 percent true to your word.

Loyalty

Our society has a skewed sense of loyalty. We know we have gone downhill when people are more committed to a

TV program, video game, or the latest piece of technology than they are to their spouse or even their job. How many of you can relate to a coworker skipping out on work, a day when you could definitely have used their help, because they were in line to buy the newest iPhone or the latest version of some steal, kill, and destroy video game? Obviously, for an organization to accomplish its goals and objectives, it needs people who are loyal to its vision. The Bible says, "Where there is no vision, the people perish" (Proverbs 29:18 KJV). Once a church or organization has a vision, it is up to each one of its followers or members to do their part to help fulfill it.

Joshua, Moses' successor as leader of the Israelites, made a rousing speech to his followers, giving a history of the great things that God had done for them over the years. Then he encouraged them to be loyal and to choose whom they would serve—foreign gods or the Lord God. Joshua set the example by saying, "As for me and my house, we will serve the Lord" (Joshua 24:15 NKJV). If the Israelites had not seen how loyal Joshua was to both Moses and God over the years, his statement would not have been near as effective. Instead, it strengthened the Israelites loyalty to the Lord as they vowed to stand with him and serve God too (Joshua 24:24).

In contrast, Satan's pride got the best of him, and he wound up aspiring to be above God. We know that this didn't work out well for him, certainly a motivating factor for us to remain loyal to God's leadership (Isaiah 14:12–15).

If you have been placed in a position of leadership in your church or organization, understand that loyalty is an important factor on the journey to success. If I feel a person in my company is not loyal to where we are going, that individual is not going to stay in leadership for long. Common sense would ask, "Why would we promote someone who is not loyal to God and what we are doing as an organization?" And the grand prize answer is—we wouldn't. Loyalty becomes self-evident. Eventually, people's words and actions reveal whether or not they are loyal to what the organization is doing.

I have had the honor of working with an amazing group of people for years. I believe I receive loyalty from my team because they ultimately know I am totally loyal to them. I tell all my staff from top to bottom, "You have my personal cell phone number. If you ever have a problem, you can call me. I am available twenty-four hours a day." I have had people call in the middle of the night with major issues, and I am so glad they did. I have never had anyone misuse the privilege. If you are going to accept the responsibility of a position of leadership within your church or company, get behind the vision of the organization, and inspire those under you to do the same.

Teachable

Another godly trait that reaps amazing results in our individual lives is being teachable. In historic times, it was very common for someone to apprentice before they became a craftsman. I'm sure Jesus even had to be teachable when He was learning carpentry from His stepdad, Joseph. Jesus could have said, "Hey, do you know who I am? I was here before you. I was the Word that became flesh. I will show you how to build some real furniture!"

Two of the greatest Old Testament leaders, Moses and David, heeded God's wisdom and guidance in their lives.

I didn't say they always did things the right way, but even when they messed up (like we all have), they both continued to seek God and follow His guidance (Numbers 20:8–29; 2 Samuel 12:1–14). Think about how David worshiped God with so much zeal that God called him "a man after His own heart" (1 Samuel 13:14, 2 Samuel 6:16-22). Both men continued to submit themselves and learn from God. There are many people in our lives from whom we can learn. We can learn from others' mistakes, as well as their successes. I have friends who have great marriages, others who have a great relationship with God, and others with successful businesses. I can learn how to become successful in many different facets of life from these friends and many other people I meet, if I remain teachable.

We're told in God's Word, "The way of a fool is right in his own eyes, but he who heeds counsel is wise" (Proverbs 12:15, NKJV). If we are going to continue to grow as leaders, we need to humble ourselves enough to recognize that we don't know it all and learn from those who are more knowledgeable. There are so many great things to learn and ways that this knowledge can create shortcuts for our success, if we'll just have a teachable mind-set and be willing to learn from others.

Attitude

Years ago author and motivational speaker Zig Ziglar stated, "Your attitude, not your aptitude, will determine your altitude."[8] This is a great concept because it's our own attitude that determines what we achieve in life. What is our attitude about going to church every week? What is our attitude about reading God's Word? What is our attitude about serving? As a leader, I'm not likely to expand people's responsibilities or roles in my organization if they have a lousy attitude, even if they're extremely competent.

A bad attitude can permeate and cause extensive damage to coworkers or group members, leading to lower productivity, higher turnover, inferior service, and so on. In a church, a poor attitude may be even more glaringly obvious and can have eternal consequences. A newcomer may never set foot in a church again because they ran into a rude usher who was grumpy because he had to get to church early. Don't be that person! Instead think, "This is the day the Lord has made; [I] will rejoice and be glad in it" (Psalm 118:24, NKJV). Work and serve with joy, and see your success soar.

Serve to Lead

Jesus seemed to have one overarching viewpoint on leadership, which is that we should serve others. The greatest leader is the greatest servant (Mark 10:42–45; Luke 22:27; John 13:1–17). I recently met a couple who came to a class I was teaching for new church attendees that helped them get acquainted with the church's beliefs and doctrine. The husband boldly stepped up after class and said that he didn't do menial serving things; his calling was to leadership. He said, "I have been to too many churches and they always want me to serve, but I quit going to them. I'm not here to serve people. I have prayed about it, and I believe God told me to come here and tell you how to lead this church. You and the pastor should listen to my advice."

I thought this was an interesting approach for a new attendee, to start by wanting to lead the church. I expressed our viewpoint that if you're not willing to serve, it disqualifies you to lead. I never saw them again. If Jesus, God's own Son, "did not come to be served, but to serve, and to give His life a ransom for many" (Mark 10:45, NKJV), then it seems to me that we have the perfect example of how a great leader should be a great servant as well.

Lending a Hand

Chances are, your pastor could use some help serving. What if we took on the attitude that we are partnering with our pastors to impact the world for Christ instead of just being a member of the church? What if we saw ourselves as part of the body of Christ, meaning that it was our individual responsibility to reflect the loving nature of Jesus, so we looked for ways to fulfill this purpose? The pastor is doing his part, and it takes the rest of us collaborating with him to maximize our results. What if it were of paramount importance for us to fulfill our role, whether in ushering, cleaning the bathrooms, or copying bulletins? Regardless of our position, we are all strategically important in making up the complete body of Christ (Colossians 1:18).

Think of the human body and all of the cells it is comprised of. Scientists estimate the average body to have 37.2 trillion cells (man, am I glad I didn't get the job of counting them), and there are an estimated 2.4 billion Christians in the world. Just like the cells in the body, everyone is important, regardless of whether or not they think so. You and I are vitally important, no matter what seemingly unimportant role we fill (1 Corinthians 12:12–31). We all need to faithfully do our part to make sure the body of Christ functions in a healthy manner.

There is a different mentality when our viewpoint is unity and partnership. I have had church attendees come up to me and say, "Mac, the garbage is full in the ladies' bathroom." I say, "Cool, are you part of the body of Christ? Are you walking in unity? If so, why are you wasting time telling me about a full garbage can? Why don't you just empty it?" (Of course, I say this with a smile on my face and in a warm tone of voice). I have taught this example repeatedly, and it has had a ripple effect throughout the church. I recently saw a lady walking down the hall with a roll of toilet paper in her hand. She smiled with a twinkle in her eye and proudly held up the roll saying, "I'm a partner!" as she walked toward the women's bathroom.

Promotion

Thankfully, the attitude of "I'm here to serve" is very normal in a healthy, growing church. Many people understand it is about using our gifts and abilities to help the church move forward. Most churches (and organizations) are looking for many of the traits we have just discussed: faithfulness, accountability, a teachable attitude, and a willingness to serve. Typically, regardless of how long you have been attending the church, you're not going to be placed in a position of leadership at the outset. You need to prove yourself. Start out by volunteering in an area where you are both talented and passionate. Next, be completely trustworthy in handling that area. It sounds simple, but show up when you say you are going to do so, on time, and be prepared. However big or small the ministry role may seem, don't assume you're not needed and flake out. Someone else will have to pick up the slack.

If you can demonstrate that you're dependable and can manage people, you may gradually be asked to take on a larger leadership role in that area. If I'm looking to hire or promote, I normally look to people I know who have already proven themselves instead of someone who has no track record with me.

MAC MAYER

Task versus People

When developing your leadership skills, one area of self-awareness that can help tremendously is understanding whether you're more task-oriented or people-oriented. Task-oriented personalities focus on getting the job done, productivity, and efficiency. These people are list makers with concrete goals and daily jobs they want to accomplish. People-oriented personalities focus more on building relationships, meeting people's needs, and caring more about the feelings of people around them rather than accomplishing specific tasks or goals. Think Mary and Martha in the Bible when Jesus stopped by for dinner (Luke 10:38–42). Mary was all about hanging out with Jesus (people), and Martha had her focus on kitchen work and actually getting the meal to the table (task).

We all process things differently. I have always been very task-oriented. Growing up in a strong German family, there was almost zero expression of love shown, but there was a gigantic focus on production. My father was a workaholic, alcoholic, and just about any other kind of "holic." Everything was about work. As previously mentioned, I started my first real job at twelve years old. At that time in history, it was less about how old you were and more about finding people who were willing to work. For low-paying, less desirable jobs, employers could hire teenagers or, in my case, a preteen. By the time I was in high school, I had three jobs, plus I would occasionally show up for school.

For me, being immensely task-oriented had both its positive and negative aspects. The positive was that through some crazy circumstances at the age of eighteen, I started a real estate appraisal company, not knowing anything about

WELL DONE

appraisals or real estate. What eventually made the company successful was I charged a third of the price that typical appraisal companies charged, and I promised a twenty-four-hour turnaround time on all my work. The task-oriented side of me stayed up most nights, sticking to my promise of delivering each report in twenty-four hours. Things worked fine until I started hiring staff. Oddly enough, they didn't like working twenty-four-hour days and made up lame excuses like seeing their families, sleeping, and other such nonsense to avoid work. My overly task-oriented personality made me a night-*Mayer* of an employer.

Years later I learned the key to making things work, and I altered my extreme work expectations. After I became a Christian, I changed my extreme obsession with completing jobs and focused more on the task of loving people. I mean, that is what Jesus commanded us to do, right? "You shall love your neighbor as yourself" (Mark 12:31, NKJV). I know this may sound crazy to you high task-oriented people, but when I genuinely made my *task* loving, encouraging, and caring for others—not out of manipulation but because I felt it was what Jesus would have me do—things changed substantially. I got along better with people, staff turnover decreased to nearly zero in my office, we got more work done sooner with fewer problems, and production skyrocketed. Imagine that! So for all of us task-oriented people, let's make our greatest task loving others.

You people-oriented folks aren't off the hook though. We're not given any specifics, but maybe Contestant #3 was hanging out with his friends after the Host left instead of developing his talents. We do know that he wasn't accomplishing the task he had been given. As we read, his excuses didn't cut it. Talking about accomplishing something and actually doing it are two different things. Let's strive to have balance and walk in love toward others while completing our godly tasks and assignments.

Decide to Be a Leader

I had been with my pastor for many years and I was devoted to helping him succeed. After thinking and praying about how I could support his successes, I decided to take the next step. As I was talking with him one day, I made the comment, "I'm your new right-hand man." Almost shocked (I seem to get that reaction from a lot of people), he said, "Mac, I have never said that." I laughed and looked around and said, "No, of course you didn't. I did. Didn't you just hear me? I am right here and just said I was your new right-hand man." I thought, *Wow! Pastor is working too hard. He really needs me if he's having a problem deciphering whether it's him speaking or me.* It was my viewpoint that if he needed something, I was there to serve him. With or without a title, it's up to each one of us to determine what our behaviors will be and whether we will be a leader, a willing follower, or both.

Lowest Leadership

I was always taught that the lowest form of leadership is using your title to get people to follow your commands. "You should do what I say because I have this title or position." This is terrible leadership. It's like having a dog that will only stay with you because you have a rope around its neck and threaten it. Wouldn't it be better if you loved the dog and he loved you and together you functioned out of love? Look at Jesus. He never made anyone follow Him and He was the Son of God, the Messiah. Real leadership occurs when people actively choose to follow us.

WELL DONE

Just thinking of leaders who have to use their title to make people follow them makes me throw up in the back of my mouth—it's totally gross. Successful leadership happens, at any age, when people willingly follow us because we have earned their respect. You can earn respect by serving, loving, being faithful, being a good example, and so on. Then when you say something, people will listen to you because you have earned their esteem, not because you have to show everyone your business card or have "leader" tattooed on your forehead.

Example

Some people (especially those who like titles) appear to have the mistaken impression that leadership is sitting in a big, cushy chair and ordering people around. True leadership could not be further from this picture. Leadership is not only a state of mind, it's also about being an example. In the early days of building companies, I determined that I was going to model my expectations for my workers. I was going to set the example of hard work, customer service, and diligence.

As I was growing up, one of my mentors said, "Whatever you do right, the people who follow you will do half of it, and whatever you do wrong, they will double." I found the last half of this principle to be just as true as the first when I went through a phase where I became very negative about our industry having unrealistic governmental demands. I found myself very pessimistic and speaking poorly about our customers. Guess what happened. You're right! The staff started to follow my not-so-positive lead, and they actually excelled at the negativity. I figured out what was going on and once again, I was the source of the problem and the key to the solution. I called a quick staff meeting, apologized for my wrong behavior, and asked the staff to correct me anytime they heard me speaking negatively about our profession. Almost immediately, our whole office made the correction, and we were on our way again in a happier environment.

I believe in serving my staff so much that in almost every major conversation, I ask them, "What do you need from me? How can I help you? Is there something I can do to help you in this process?" At the end of many conversations, I say, "I want you to promise me that if you need something you will ask me." I have to continue to remain in a position of a servant leader if I want to understand and interact with them effectively.

Communication

As previously mentioned, a leader must be someone who serves and sets the example for what he or she expects, in both word and action. Part of setting the example involves being an excellent communicator. Effective communication is so crucial to success that it's no wonder that one of the greatest war strategies is to take out the communication system of the opponent. Successful leaders must have great communication with their team, continually talking about where they are going and how they'll get there so their teammates can see where they're leading them.

A real leader doesn't normally say, "Do this because I said so." It's good to explain how and why I make decisions that affect the organization, because I want my team to know my thought process. If they understand my approach, they will be able to make decisions using this same method. I know that I'm making progress as a leader when they are repeating the guidelines that I have taught them for decision-making. Before long, I find that they're giving me great insights and solving problems on their own, using the guidelines that I've modeled and spoken repeatedly to them.

Control/Empowerment

As a young leader, not only was I overly task-oriented, which drove my staff crazy, I was also an immensely controlling micromanager, just to ensure my employees were totally abused. I justified my micromanagement under the pretense that I was being a good steward and following up to make sure every "i" was dotted. What I didn't understand was that I wasn't empowering my people to grow, make their own decisions, and learn from their outcomes, which sometimes resulted in larger or unnecessary mistakes. My controlling nature was not based on love, rather on fear. *What if they make a mistake? What if it costs us money? What if they make an embarrassment out of the company?* What if, what if, what if?

When God created the world, He did so with order. He didn't do it out of control, or things would've been exceptionally different with Adam and Eve. God did not control Adam and Eve by putting up a high-voltage fence around the Tree of Life with razor wire, vicious dogs, and a gun turret. There is a big difference between controlling everyone out of fear by disallowing staff to make decisions without seven levels of approval, and walking in love by developing an empowering organization where employees have the freedom to make decisions based on a set of core values. As a leader, I needed to learn to teach the process and values to my staff, letting them make decisions and coaching them forward from the results. It is a refreshing way to live, believing the best in people and helping them in the process of growth.

Following this method, I start out by giving my staff small responsibilities. As I see that they successfully handle these tasks, I give them more opportunities. If I ultimately get burned, which rarely happens, my goal is to stay in a position of love. The default is always, *What would love do?*

Leaders Wanted

Today, there is a deficit of real leaders. In order to make a lasting, positive effect in our communities, some of us need to step up to leadership. Jesus was the hallmark example of a servant leader. You never saw Him proclaiming His title. It was all about earned leadership by helping His followers to true success. People are looking for leaders who are real, and "practice what they preach." Remember, leadership is a mind-set. Will you take the necessary steps to earn the respect of others and lead them?

When Jesus left the earth, He instructed His followers to make disciples of all the nations (Matthew 28:19). Paul, an avid follower of Christ's teachings and author of many New Testament books, indicated that Jesus' followers are "members of [Christ's] body, and we are instructed to "not forsak[e] the assembling of ourselves together" (Hebrews 10:25, NKJV). Paul wrote to several local churches, encouraging and instructing them in the ways of God, including giving them the qualifications of a pastor (1 Timothy 3:1–7).

One thing that all effective leaders have is a mentor, an experienced or trusted advisor. This is to ensure that we stay focused and remain on a growth track. As Christians, one advisor that we should have is our pastor. A pastor is responsible for leading and teaching a group of believers. This is a critical position, not only highly respected by God, but it is also held to a higher level of accountability. There are many pitfalls and misconceptions about this area of leadership. We will have some fun and bring a little reality to the subject of pastors and our intended relationship with them in the next chapter.

Reflection Questions

1. How are you serving in your local church? In what ways can you partner with the vision expressed?

2. Are you more task-oriented (productivity) or people-oriented (relationships)?

3. If you tend to one extreme or the other, how can you bring more balance to your leadership style?

4. Who currently serves as a mentor in your life? Who are you mentoring? How can you further develop those relationships?

Chapter 9—Pastors

If we claim to love God, we must also love, honor, and submit to those He has placed in leadership positions. Failing to honor and submit to authority is a major trap that Satan uses, especially within the church, to bring disunity and draw people away from hearing the truth and serving others. Due to its critical nature and relevancy to hearing "Well done," we'll take this chapter to expound on this important topic. However, I promise that we'll continue to have an enjoyable time learning more about those whom God has appointed to lead the church—pastors.

First, I want to alert you in advance that I'm using the pronoun "he" all the way through this section when writing about pastors. I know what you are thinking, that I am a misguided person who is living in the dark ages. I acknowledge that there are many amazing, ordained women pastors, and I totally recognize the gifting of women in the body of Christ. However, writing "he/she" is a bit cumbersome and breaks up the sentence flow, so I apologize in advance. Actually, I know you have to forgive me since you can't be offended or you'll have to go back and reread chapter 4.

Pastors

Pastors have one of the toughest jobs of all time. The Bible says that not all should teach because they will be held to a higher level of accountability (James 3:1–2). Pastors take on the overwhelming responsibility of being the shepherd to their flock, the church that is made up of people from all ages, backgrounds, cultures, and viewpoints. Think of the vast spectrum of situations these people face. What if you were the one they were all looking to for solutions? What if you were responsible for trying to relate to all these different personalities, helping them grow in their relationship with God and walking out the Christian life? That sounds like an extremely challenging assignment. But wait! As their pastor, you will also be the one ultimately accountable to God for what they are being taught. This doesn't exactly make me want to run toward the front of the pastoral line yelling, "Pick me! Pick me!" Joining the circus sounds like a MUCH better idea.

The Ugly Truth

While it is a privilege to be called by God to lead the church, the truth is that the job of a pastor is not as glamorous as one would think. The following are recent statistics about pastors from the Pastoral Care Inc. website:

- Ninety percent report working fifty-five to seventy-five hours a week.
- Eighty percent believe pastoral ministry has negatively affected their families.
- Seventy percent consistently fight depression.
- Seventy percent feel grossly underpaid.
- Forty percent report serious conflict with a parishioner at least once a month.
- Fifty percent feel so discouraged they would leave the ministry if they felt they could but have no other way of making a living elsewhere.

- The profession of "Pastor" is near the bottom of a survey of the most-respected professions, just above "car salesman."[9]

With all the long hours and strains that their job puts on their personal life, it's no surprise that 1,700 pastors quit the ministry each month in 2015.[10] You may ask, "But they knew it wouldn't be a walk in the park, so why would they leave God's calling on their life?" The number-one reason pastors quit is that the church body is not willing to go in the same direction the pastor feels God is leading them.

Okay, I'm depressed just reporting these figures, let alone actually considering pastoring on a daily basis. *Where did I put my circus performer application?* Maybe we should cut these individuals and their families a little slack and look at them through a more realistic lens. Sometimes it's hard for us to understand, but pastors are people, just like you and me. My first impression of pastors was that they had a cushy job. I mean what do they really do? Get up when they want, spend some time in prayer, hang out with some friends, and then deliver a short talk once a week that they probably got from a book of sermons off Amazon.com. I mean, how tough could it be?

My whole perception changed when I actually worked in a church office. Wow, was I wrong. Talk about maxing the stress meter! It seemed like I was at Grand Central Station.

"Hey, there is a call on line one. Mrs. Wilson fell and they are taking her to the emergency room. You need to head over there to pray for her. By the way, there is a suicidal man in the waiting room. Maybe you could talk with him on your drive to see Mrs. Wilson? Also, the Smiths need marriage counseling because they had another big fight last night. Mr.

Jackson called and wants you to clearly explain the book of Revelation to him or he is leaving the church. You are scheduled to meet with him in an hour. Did I mention there is a leak in the roof over the nursery? How do you want us to handle that? There are still twenty-two messages on the answering machine from last week that have all asked for you and only you to call them back, and I have a stack of mail four inches thick to handle, so try not to spend too much time driving around with the suicidal guy and Mrs. Wilson. Also, don't forget you're preaching three times this week. The youth pastor is taking the weekend off, so that service also needs covered."

Just working at a church, as an innocent bystander, made me want to check myself into a facility with densely padded, soundproof walls, while under heavy sedation in a very remote location.

Judgment

As you can see, it's not easy being a pastor. On top of all of these responsibilities, these men and women of God and their families are some of the most judged people on the face of the earth. I'm surprised they don't all wear a disguise, with fake glasses, a rubber nose, and a sombrero pulled down over their faces, or only come out in the middle of the night when they are less likely to be recognized.

Let's say the pastor is picking up some groceries on the way home from the office and runs into some congregants at the grocery store. There could be a multitude of judgmental questions rocketing through the wide-open spaces of their minds. *Hey, it's only 4:45 p.m. Why isn't he still at his office praying for me and working on sermons? Wow, I wish I had such an easy job.* The next thing they observe is what's in the pastor's shopping cart, and the judgment continues. *I can't believe the things in his cart. And he says we should be good stewards! Is that a bag of Oreos I see peeking out from under the bundle of toilet paper? I don't think he should be eating Oreos. After all, doesn't the Bible say our bodies are a temple? Is that ice cream too? I know one thing—his kids certainly don't need any more sugar.* Then when the pastor is going through the checkout line, the scrutiny continues. *He didn't even lead that unfortunate girl at the checkout counter in the sinner's prayer. Now she'll probably end up in hell, all because of him. And he says we should care about the unsaved in our city! What a hypocrite.*

If the pastor's house has a well-maintained lawn, we wonder why he's spending his resources on such an insignificant, worldly thing as a lawn when he could be praying and seeking the lost. If the pastor's lawn is a little overgrown or unkempt, we condemn him for being a bad example to his neighbors. If the pastor has a big house or a nice car, especially if it's bigger or nicer than ours, a whole host of less-than-remarkable thoughts come to our minds like, *He's stealing the offering.* I purposely make these examples sound overly exaggerated. Yet the crazy thing is that these accusations and many more are continually brought against pastors and their families. Judgment against pastors and those in leadership positions is the devil's trap to diminish their credibility and authority in the church.

Mistakes

I'm not saying that pastors are perfect. They *are* human after all. Sure, pastors have made and will continue to make mistakes. The issue is not whether your pastor has made mistakes; it's where your heart is in relation to your pastor and his family.

WELL DONE

If we're not seeing issues from a position of love, we're wrong. We serve an all-knowing God who is aware of everything that is going on in our lives (Job 34:21). He knows every thought and every action behind every closed door. God functions from a position of love, and I'm so thankful He does. Trust me, God is more than capable of exposing or bringing to account any wayward church leadership. It's just a matter of time.

If we bring accusations against those God has put in authority, it puts us in a very precarious position because He will defend their position of leadership. Look at the story of Aaron and Miriam when they spoke against Moses. "Then Miriam and Aaron spoke against Moses because of the Ethiopian woman whom he had married; for he had married an Ethiopian woman" (Numbers 12:1, NKJV). However, God was quick to defend Moses. Within the next few verses, we see that He called all three of them outside and reprimanded the two who had spoken against His chosen leader. But He didn't stop there. As we keep reading it says,

> So the anger of the LORD WAS AROUSED AGAINST THEM, AND HE DEPARTED. And when the cloud departed from above the tabernacle, suddenly Miriam became leprous, as white as snow. Then Aaron turned toward Miriam, and there she was, a leper. So Aaron said to Moses, "Oh, my lord! Please do not lay this sin on us, in which we have done foolishly and in which we have sinned. Please do not let her be as one dead, whose flesh is half consumed when he comes out of his mother's womb!" (Numbers 12:9–12, NKJV)

It was only after Moses prayed on Miriam's behalf that she recovered from leprosy. God obviously takes speaking against His chosen people very seriously.

Based on this example, we see that God doesn't take kindly to authority figures being bad-mouthed. It's in our best interest to avoid this trap and align ourselves with God's chosen leaders rather than against them. *Father, I honor the position of authority in which You placed them, and I will not speak against Your leadership. If they're not honoring You and You want them out of their leadership position, You're going to have to do it.* I won't lift my hand or voice against God's leadership. I like my skin complexion just the way it is.

Grace

There's so much pressure and responsibility placed on pastors' shoulders that we should show an immense amount of grace and latitude toward these amazing people. Pastors are God's representatives on the earth, while living in a glass box for the entire world to judge their every move and motive. The church's job is to honor, bless, and pray for these leaders that God gives to us, casting away our scrutiny and extending God's love and grace to them and their families.

Pray for Your Pastor

The number-one thing we can do for our pastors and their families is to pray for them. I'd recommend you continually pray for the leadership in your life. It's not only biblical, it's just common sense (1 Timothy 2:2). If I'm riding in a car, I want the person in the driver's seat to do really, really well. I hope that person is alert, protected, and hearing from God about things going on up the road. Why? Because I want to arrive at my destination safely! That's why I feel it's vital that we're praying for our pastors and those in a position of influence in our churches. I want them and their families blessed, attentive to God, and under His protective covering because

WELL DONE

my family and I are in the "church car" and the pastor is driving. Pray for all the leadership in your life regularly. Pray for your government officials, pray for your boss, and most importantly pray for your pastors and their families.

Look at it this way. In any combat situation, if an enemy can remove their opponent's leadership in some way, it's easier to defeat their troops. This tactic is called, "cutting off the head of the snake." Just think, if Satan had been successful in his temptations of Jesus, we all would be up the proverbial creek without a paddle. Yet he didn't stop with just trying to take out Jesus. Now he has his sights set on those who lead His flock.

Enemy fire comes in many forms at pastors and their families, from sickness and disease, to wayward kids, to all forms of temptation. All sizes of churches and ministries are under the attack of Satan. We don't hear about all the smaller ministries that get pounded, but they do. And think of the number of high-profile pastors and ministry leaders who have fallen over the years and the havoc that has been wrought with untold thousands of followers.

My heart goes out to the pastoral families who are caught in this real-world, high-powered spiritual crossfire. On one side, they have all the demonic forces of hell trying to take them out so their flock will be in turmoil. On the other side, they have a disrespecting, condescending, and deteriorating world mocking or disregarding them. A pastor's safe haven should be his understanding and supportive church family. Unfortunately, many pastors are ambushed by what could only be termed friendly fire, eliminated by their own congregation. That's why it's so important for us to adamantly resolve to support and fervently pray for our pastors and their families.

MAC MAYER

Relating to Pastors

If I love and support my pastor unconditionally, pretty soon he's going to understand that I'm not trying to stab him in the back, split his church, or any of the other divisive things he's experienced over the last month. Just by me loving and serving him, he'll be able to relax and grow as well.

It seems everyone wants to tell the pastor or leadership what they're doing wrong. "Hey, you misquoted that verse." "Your fly was down during the whole service today." "You look like you didn't get enough sleep." Do you know how deflating that can be? Some pastors even get to the point where they hate to open their e-mails, because they know they're going to get blasted by their own parishioners.

I know this is crazy, but what if we were "good-finders," and we looked for things our pastors did right and complimented them? Wow, that would be a refreshing reversal! The Bible actually says, "Let the elders who rule well be counted worthy of double honor, especially those who labor in the word and doctrine" (1 Timothy 5:17, NKJV). I'm not making this up, folks.

Honor

In fact, the Bible places a rather strong emphasis on honoring leadership. Look at the story of David and King Saul (1 Samuel 15–26). As the king of Israel, Saul seemed to make one bad decision after another. Yet David still showed respect for Saul's position of authority, even though David had been chosen to replace him. Saul was in the wrong, but David honored him. Even though he had multiple opportunities to retaliate, he didn't take them.

WELL DONE

God could've been giving Saul a chance to repent and handle things properly. He also could've been fully checking out David's heart. God could've been thinking, *I wonder if David will continue to honor and stay in correct relationship to authority if I place King Saul next to him, defenseless in a cave, with his trousers down around his ankles?* It totally looked like God had delivered Saul to him. "Look David, here is vulnerable King Saul, at your cave door, ready for you to stab your sword into him. Now, you can walk into your rightful kingship."

This wasn't an easy decision. David knew that with a quick thrust of the sword, he could go back and live in luxury at the palace as the anointed and prophesied king. Or he could remain in a position of honor toward Saul's authority and continue living as an outcast in the blazing, hot desert with a bunch of smelly, misfit followers foraging to stay alive.

Whether a person is the head of a family, head of a company, head of a church, or head of our nation, we need to show honor to them because of the position they hold. This doesn't mean we have to agree with everything they say or do. The leader could be making frequent, uninformed, or careless decisions, but we are still called to honor the position. If God wants to discipline His leadership, He knows their address and it's up to Him to do so (Romans 13:1–7).

If our default is love and honor, we will always be right. Remember, Saul turned his back on God and was 100 percent in the wrong, and David was the newly anointed king of Israel and appeared to be 100 percent in the right (1 Samuel 15:10–11, 16:13). However, if David had come against Saul, he would've been absolutely wrong. Let's follow David's example and determine to always honor those who are in a position of authority in our lives, regardless of their actions. By doing this, we will be honoring God.

Thinking the Best

Part of honoring those in positions of authority means giving them the benefit of the doubt, even when we're not privy to details we think we have a right to know. Working behind the scenes with pastors, I see the many difficult decisions they have to make. Unfortunately, due to confidentiality and to protect the parties involved, these leaders generally cannot share the rationale behind their decisions.

Just recently, I had to make a very tough decision to fire someone on a church staff who had been a very diligent worker and was wonderfully liked by their coworkers. I had personally hired the individual and was glad to have done so. However, something major happened and I had to be the one responsible for letting the staff member go. You can imagine the controversy that could've happened among the staff. I told them, "Look, you know I love this person, and in fairness to the person being fired, I will not discuss the situation." There are just things that a leader knows that they cannot, out of good conscience, share with others.

From my standpoint as an employer, I still believe the best in my employees and will do everything I can to help them move forward in life. I expect the team to believe the best about the person who was fired *and* to believe the best about those who made the decision. *Look, we know our leaders. They are very fair and loving, and they wouldn't have fired the person unless they had substantial cause.* And that's just how the staff reacted. We have to think the best.

"But Mac, what about all of those preachers and companies who were dishonest or immoral? Shouldn't there be transparency to keep them accountable?" Of course, churches and companies should be as open with their congregants and stakeholders as possible, but there is always more to the situation than we see. Because of discretion, there are things that can't be shared. If there is clear evidence of misbehavior in the leadership, we should pray for the Lord's leading to address the situation in a loving manner (Ephesians 4:15).

While situations like this occur, they're not as prevalent as the world and media would like us to believe. If we feel the Lord's calling to be a part of a certain church or work at a certain company, then we need to think the best about the leadership, be sensitive to God's guidance, and leave the rest up to God. Remember, the answer to our behavior in all situations is to ask the question, *What would love do?* Leaders have to make many difficult decisions on a regular basis, and they can't stop to broadcast their entire thought process. This is another prime reason why we need to continue to pray fervently for our church leadership.

Pastors and New Ideas

Remember the previous statistics about pastors that were presented at the beginning of the chapter? The number-one reason pastors quit is that the church body isn't willing to go in the same direction the pastor feels God is leading them. This means the pastor is trying to move some ideas forward, and the congregation throws a proverbial fit. Pastors should be commended for trying new ideas, even if they fail. Everything in a church is designed to stay static. *By golly, we have done this since Columbus came to the U.S., so why change a thing?* Any pastor who is willing to change things for the better should be applauded and supported, even if it doesn't work out.

My heart goes out to the first pastor who wanted to try my ideas for church growth. After several months of working with this pastor and seeing success, he said, "Mac, we want to hire you and move forward with your viewpoints." I stood there in shock. As you can see, I think a little bit differently and to have a pastor who was willing to risk his reputation by using my ideas to impact lives for the kingdom was humbling.

I really like this pastor, but one side of me totally questioned his mental faculties—*What is your congregation going to think?* It's strange when you're concerned for someone after they just made the decision to hire you. This was a huge decision on his part. If the ideas didn't work, I could just slither out of the church scarcely noticed and leave town. The pastor couldn't skip out. He would be left to answer questions by his congregation about why he let that guy with the new ideas mess with their dormant church. Thank you, Lord, the ideas worked, and the church experienced wonderful, healthy growth!

If we want to seriously increase the kingdom of God and see more people set free, not only do we need to support our pastors but we also need to support other church bodies. It is essential that we work together for two reasons: (1) God commanded us to walk in unity, and (2) we will all be together for eternity, so we might as well work together now. If we want to accomplish more for the kingdom of God, we need to see how we can team up with other groups of believers.

Reflection Questions

1. Do you consistently pray for your pastor and others in positions of authority?

2. Have you ever found yourself dishonoring your pastor or those in authority? How did you remedy that situation?

3. What can you do to help your pastor feel more loved and appreciated?

Chapter 10—Some Final Thoughts: Team Up to Win!

It's interesting to me that often when we talk about uniting Christians, automatically we think of groups that we have nothing in common with except confessing Christ. These are the groups on the opposite side of the spectrum from our beliefs, and we can't imagine working with them. I understand your thoughts, and may I suggest reading 1 Corinthians 1:10–17? Within this section, Paul discourages this type of division among believers.

Unity Basics

The unity Jesus indicated starts on a basic level. Before we can be unified in the global body of Christ, we need to start with basic components like getting along with the people closest to us. This could mean living in harmony with our spouse and family. Next, we need to strive to be unified within our churches.

As I mentioned, too many people are looking for things to argue about with their spouse, their pastor, and other churches. Instead of looking at areas in which we disagree, what if we looked at how we could agree more with each other? What if we had the mentality of a TEAM, where Together Everyone Accomplishes More? If we are going to impact this world in a meaningful way, it's not going to be by acting like the Lone Ranger and wandering off through the desert on our white horse, Silver, looking for bad people. The Father knew it would take a combined effort of us working together to make maximum impact. To do this, we need to unite with others who proclaim the name of Jesus as Lord.

Competition

While we should be walking in unity, many churches adopt the world's sense of competition: functioning as rival corporations rather than a place where people can come to feel God's love and presence. When I was growing up in the competitive business world, I had to decide what viewpoint I would have toward competing companies. Naturally, my highly competitive personality won over, and I carried this mind-set into my business practices. My viewpoint was, *Let's do a great job and put them all out of business.* This seemed like a sensible thought from a moneymaking perspective. Drive them all out of business, and we get all the customers. How could a goal be any clearer? However when I thought about it, I didn't like the gross, mildly nauseous feeling it gave me.

During a time when I was experiencing problems with some new technology, I happened to run into one of my archrivals, whom I had positioned in my mind as one of the business antichrists that I wanted to run out of business. In one conversation with him, he mentioned that he knew the answer to our problem and he would be glad to come by to help us, which he did. Talk about a gut check! He seemed so happy and willing to help us in several areas. I later found out he was a Christian, and his loving conduct spoke volumes to me.

It was because of amazing businessmen like Ken, Ralph, and Hutch, who continued to model a different way of life for me, that I changed my business perspective. I was so impressed with them that I adopted their philosophy in our company. Yes, we worked hard, but my focus turned from putting my competition out of business to better serving my clients. We also decided as a company that if any of our competition needed help, we would willingly pass on any information and help them in any way we could. This may have cost us some business; I'm not sure, but truthfully I don't care. I was at peace with the way we operated the company and how we interacted with others in our industry, even competitors.

In the body of Christ, how much more gracious and helpful toward other Christians and churches should our attitude be? We're not in competition—we're on the same team. If we can share any information that will help other churches to succeed, we should willingly do it because it's not about us; it's about sharing God's love with those who need to hear it.

Satan Wants to Divide and Conquer

Being unified is not just a nice phrase; it's a matter of survival!

Understand that Satan comes to steal, kill, and destroy (John 10:10). The easiest way for him to be successful is to get you away from your fellow believers. You know the strategy of a wolf. A wolf's goal is to get an animal anxious and confused, so it will be separated from the herd and easier to devour by the snarling pack of wolves. If you stay secure in the middle of the pack, you will be much more secure and supported so you cannot be ripped to shreds by gnashing teeth.

WELL DONE

With a dysfunctional upbringing and poor choices while growing up, it shouldn't be surprising that my group of friends was less than desirable. In fact, many of my childhood friends died young, and my best friend went to prison multiple times until I lost track of him. When I accepted the Lord as an adult through my business connections, I hung on to salvation and my new group of Christian friends like a life preserver. I'm not saying it was right, but I was scared to miss church; I was scared to be separated from the safety net of my church herd.

Over the years, I've seen many friends become casual about going to church and in their relationship with God. "Yep, I'll go to church if there's nothing on TV, if I get up on time, and if I can't come up with anything else to do." These people are much braver than I am, and unfortunately, many of them have become lukewarm or deceived and walked away from their faith, playing into the wolf's strategy.

Perhaps you're familiar with the analogy that a burning hot coal removed from a fireplace soon begins to darken and grow cold since it's not placed next to other burning coals. That's the way I felt—on fire and sizzling—next to my on-fire friends, but then I would pull away and that fire for God was a distant, faded black memory.

This life is too important. Let's determine that we're going to be white-hot on fire to accomplish the mission God gave us: the Great Commission (Matthew 28:19). Remember, Jesus took our place on the cross so we could take His place of impacting lives on this earth. Let's do it to the best of our abilities!

MAC MAYER

Church Unity

Just like individual believers, churches are also gifted specifically and called to fulfill and accomplish different roles for the kingdom of God, including support systems to keep their flock safe. Some churches specialize in missions, some in drama presentations, some in helping the needy, and some churches are geared toward senior citizens. I would encourage each church to excel at whatever specific ministry they were called to do.

Years ago, leaders at a more established denominational church approached me and said they wanted to change their whole structure to attract younger members. I said, "What do you want to do that for?"

They replied, "If we don't attract younger members, our church will die!" This sounds very logical, right?

I said, "No, if you try to do something your church is neither called to do nor gifted at, it will die." Here's the thing—there was nothing about this church that was appealing to young families. The building was not modern looking, they had no facilities for young families, and everything about the place was geared toward seniors.

I said, "What if you start being the very best you can be at ministering to seniors? Let other churches that are geared toward families work with them." They said, "Mac, all of these people are old and they're going to die." I responded with, "You're right and there's an endless stream of old people who are a quick bus ride away from the pearly gates of heaven. Why don't you serve them and make sure these people have their name written for eternity with Jesus before they get on the bus for their very last stop? Your church could

WELL DONE

have amazing success at serving the elderly, a demographic that you are already geared for, and substantially populating the kingdom of heaven. You could be an inspiration to other dwindling churches on how to turn things around. If you're serving this demographic right, more of them will want to come here and you can introduce them to Jesus. Yes, it'll be hard work and you might have to get innovative. You might have to get buses and drivers to pick people up and transport your members to and from doctors' appointments. You may need volunteers to sing hymns and serve meals. There are a multitude of people in the sixty-plus age range who need to hear about Jesus, and if we actively serve them, we can change their lives for eternity."

Their other option was to be something they were not, a seeker-friendly hip church, and all the old people would leave and the young families would know they were frauds and run away too. This is where prayer and wisdom come together. Remember how we talked about convergence? What can you do that is amazing and what does your market need? Now bring those two things together and hit it out of the park for the kingdom of God!

Staying true to your church's area of ministry while supporting other churches will allow God to move in ways you have only dreamed, preventing the devil from stealing your flock and seeing your church fulfill the plan that God has for their lives.

Reflection Questions

1. What actions can you take to be more unified with your natural and spiritual families?

2. How can you foster unity and cooperation with other bodies of believers in your community?

WELL DONE

Conclusion

First, I want to commend you for reading this book. It's been very fast paced, and we have covered a lot of practical information in a relatively short period of time. I'm hoping this book will take you one step closer to the ultimate goal that all Christians should yearn for—to hear, "Well done" from the Great Reality Show Host, Jesus. I've given you real steps and questions to answer in the pursuit of finding and fulfilling the call of God on your life. As part of the body of Christ, every believer has something he or she is supposed to do for the kingdom of God, and my hope and prayer is that this resource helps you accomplish that destiny.

Throughout this book, I've been very transparent about all the things I haven't been called to do, that is, music, mechanics, art, and the list goes on and on. I do know what I'm called to do, and that's helping people find what they are called to do and building teams of people to accomplish it. It has been my pleasure spending this time with you and I look forward to hearing "Well done" with you and spending eternity together with our amazing King and Father in heaven.

God's blessings on your successful journey to hearing, "Well done, thou good and faithful servant!" (Matthew 25:21, KJV).

Your teammate,

Mac

Notes

Chapter 2

1. *Webster's Dictionary 1828 Online*, s.v. "meditate," accessed August 2, 2016, http://webstersdictionary1828.com/Dictionary/meditate.

Chapter 4

2. *Bibleapps.com*, s.v. "skandalon," Thayer's Greek Lexicon, accessed November 7, 2016, http://bibleapps.com/greek/4625.htm.

Chapter 5

3. *City Slickers*, IMDB, accessed October 30, 2016, http://www.imdb.com/title/tt0101587/quotes.
4. *Wikipedia*, s.v. "Peter principle," accessed October 30, 2016, https://en.wikipedia.org/wiki/Peter_principle.

Chapter 6

5. Eric Foner and John A. Garraty, eds., *The Reader's Companion to American History* (Boston: Houghton Mifflin Harcourt, 1991).
6. Thomas Edison, The Quotations Page, accessed October 2, 2016, http://www.quotationspage.com/quote/35566.html.

Chapter 7

7. John Maxwell, The John Maxwell Co., accessed October 30, 2016, http://www.johnmaxwell.com/about/meet-john/.

Chapter 8

8. Ziglar.com, accessed October 30, 2016, https://www.ziglar.com/quotes/your-attitude-not-your-aptitude/.

Chapter 9

9. Pastoral Care Inc., "Statistics in the Ministry," accessed October 30, 2016, www.pastoralcareinc.com/statistics/.

10. Ibid.